The Vault Career Guide to
Private Wealth Management
**is made possible through the
generous support of the
following sponsors:**

VAULT CAREER GUIDE TO
PRIVATE WEALTH MANAGEMENT

VAULT CAREER GUIDE TO
PRIVATE WEALTH MANAGEMENT

MIKE MARTINEZ
AND THE STAFF OF VAULT

For information about permission to reproduce selections from this book, contact Vault Inc.,
150 West 22nd St, New York, New York 10011, (212) 366-4212.

Library of Congress CIP Data is available.

ISBN 1-58131-448-5

Printed in the United States of America

ACKNOWLEDGMENTS

We are extremely grateful to Vault's entire staff for all their help in the editorial, production and marketing processes. Vault also would like to acknowledge the support of our investors, clients, employees, family and friends. Thank you!

Your exceptional talent drives our success. It starts with you.

Our employees are what make UBS a global financial powerhouse. Their ideas, skills and commitment to excellence are the bedrock of our success. So at UBS, we offer you a world of opportunities to enable you to achieve. Every one of our offices around the globe is built on the respect and support you need to meet your potential and help you to excel. To keep you inspired we provide the best training available. From day one, we value your skills and ambition.

It starts with you: **www.ubs.com/graduates**

UBS is an equal opportunity employer committed to diversity in its workplace. (M/F/D/V)

Wealth | Global Asset | Investment
Management | Management | Bank

You & Us

Table of Contents

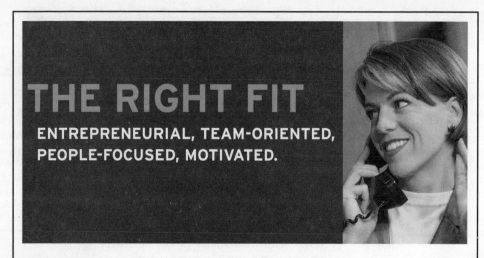

THE RIGHT FIT

ENTREPRENEURIAL, TEAM-ORIENTED, PEOPLE-FOCUSED, MOTIVATED.

The right fit. When it comes to your career, it can mean one that fits your personality, or maybe one that capitalizes on your talents or maximizes your skills. Or perhaps it's one that does all three—like a career as a Smith Barney Financial Advisor.

We're looking for a diverse group of people from a range of backgrounds to join us in a firm that is people-focused, entrepreneurial-based and growth-oriented, one that rewards individual initiative and team building. If this sounds like your goal, we may have the perfect fit for you here.

**To find out more or to apply online, please visit
www.smithbarney.com/recruiting**

Chapter: 10 Lifestyle   87

FIRM PROFILES   95

*Employers highlighted above provided generous underwriting support for
the Vault Career Guide to Private Wealth Management.*

Employers highlighted above provided generous underwriting support for the Vault Career Guide to Private Wealth Management.

Introduction

Wealthy people come from all walks of life and make their money all sorts of ways. Some are doctors or lawyers, and others are small business owners operating roofing businesses or a chain of dry cleaners. Some inherited their wealth, and others are corporate middle-level executives who've saved and invested, making millions in the process until they became rich. And yet others are high school dropouts who started their own companies, eventually selling them for handsome sums.

No matter what their background, though, the wealthy have various asset management issues that are different than the average Joe's with a 401(k) and a few hundred stock options in the firm he works for. To address these more complex asset management issues, the financial services industry has created private wealth management departments that offer a host of products and services for the very wealthy.

Private wealth management, also called private banking, is a specialized branch of the investment community that provides one-stop shopping for a whole host of products and services needed by wealthy folks—typically defined as those who have liquid assets of more than over $1 million. But the most prestigious private banks, such as those attached to major investment companies like Citigroup, Goldman Sachs or Lehman Brothers, have much higher minimums, over $5 million in some cases, and cater to the richest of the rich.

Visit the Vault Finance Career Channel at **www.vault.com/finance** – with insider firm profiles, message boards, the Vault Finance Job Board and more.

VAULT CAREER LIBRARY

1

THE SCOOP

The Basic Functions of Wealth Management Companies

CHAPTER 1

The Basic Functions of Wealth Management Companies

Creating income

It is the first job of private wealth managers to help create, from among various investment strategies, income or growth sufficient for the everyday needs of their clients. In addition, they must provide enough excess growth to account for inflation in order that their clients' purchasing power does not become eroded over time. In addition, hopefully the wealth manager will continue to grow the clients' assets so that they become richer.

Because the wealthy often need to live solely off of their investments, today private wealth managers must use a variety of investment techniques to help clients create enough income to live off of every year. Sounds easy enough right? Not really. When you consider that someone who invests $1 million in a conservative corporate bond returning 5 percent creates a modest $50,000 a year in income, it becomes obvious that having $1 million dollars or so just isn't as big of a deal as it used to be. Sure, $50,000 is a lot of money for doing nothing, but living on champagne and caviar is out of the question. With wages in the U.S. averaging a little over $35,000 per year as of 2004, according to the Social Security Administration, the average typical family with two income-earners can make more than someone with $1 million in the bank who lives off of his or her investments. Indeed, because of inflation, the portfolio with $1 million must return in excess of 7.5 percent just to keep up with the two-worker household that can possibly expect to get raises every year. With rates of return in the stock market sometimes as high as 20 percent or more, 7.5 percent may not seem a very high return, but when you consider that the S&P 500 in the six years since 2000 has returned less than 1 percent annually, you'll see that the job of private wealth managers in creating income for their clients isn't always easy.

Paying taxes

Another problem wealthy clients often encounter is taxes. None of us likes paying taxes. For most of us, however, we would willingly pay additional taxes if it meant that we were making additional income. For the wealthy it isn't quite so simple. When managing large pools of assets, small differences in tax rates can translate into big changes in after-tax returns. Various types of investments used are treated and taxed differently by the IRS. For example, income derived from the interest rates of bonds is taxed differently than long-term capital gains derived from selling stock. It is the private wealth manager's job to balance assorted types of investments to create the most tax efficient combination for the client.

Wealthy people are also subject to inheritance taxes. Accordingly, private wealth managers must help their clients select from a number of products or legal entities, such as trusts or insurance, to preserve their estates after their death. Though the private wealth manager does not offer legal strategy (it is against the law for anyone other than a lawyer to offer legal advice), the manager must be well versed on the various laws regarding trusts and estates. Additionally, private wealth managers often have insight and experience in managing charitable investment entities, such as endowments and foundations.

Asset protection

In today's society, people with money are sometimes targeted with lawsuits just because they happen to have money. So, an increasingly popular area of practice for private wealth managers is called "asset protection," which helps the wealthy guard against losing money in civil lawsuits. There are several techniques used to protect assets, including U.S. trusts laws and foreign, off-shore banks. Advocates of asset protection methods contend that making their clients impervious to lawsuits doesn't just protect assets, but also prevents lawsuits from even happening.

Though the above are some of the main areas in which a private wealth manager will work, they are certainly not the only ones. In general, clients will often rely on advice from their private wealth managers for a variety of decisions outside of investments. Decisions ranging from what type of car to buy to which is the best kidnap insurance policy to use are often made by clients only after first consulting their private wealth managers.

In a nutshell

The private wealth management industry integrates the varied and complex business of managing wealth by accounting for income needs, taxes, estate preservation and asset protection for the wealthy. Typically, private wealth management is a smaller division of a much larger investment firm or bank. The private wealth manager leverages the expertise of the various departments inside the firm (such as the trust department) to present clients with solutions to wealth management issues. Though not required to be experts in one particular area of wealth management, private wealth managers must know enough about each area to expertly represent their clients' best interests and, where appropriate, offer advice.

Other Services Provide by Wealth Managers

The above provides a glimpse of the more common types of services that private wealth management firms offer their clients. But some firms also offer other unique services, which vary from firm to firm.

Some of these might include:

- Philanthropic services: Giving to charities in a planned way.

- Agricultural services: The transfer and or management of farms or ranches for families.

- Auction and art services: Providing services allowing clients to purchase, value, sell and manage collections of fine art.

- Appraisal services: Valuing and managing unique assets like intellectual property.

- Securitization services: Providing ways to monetize any assets that provide a stream of cash flow, like movie or book royalties.

Visit the Vault Finance Career Channel at **www.vault.com/finance** – with insider firm profiles, message boards, the Vault Finance Job Board and more.

VAULT CAREER LIBRARY

7

Financial Advisor Categories

Why all the names? What's the difference?

The three major types of financial advisors who represent the three major types of clients for an investment firm are: 1) private client representatives, (or retail brokers); 2) institutional salespeople (mutual funds, hedge funds, etc.); and 3) private wealth managers (the focus of this guide). The investment industry is a sales-driven one, with various salespeople assigned to different types of customers. Generally speaking, private client salespeople don't work with institutional accounts, for example, or vice versa. Each type of salesperson is typically an expert in the investment issues their clients face. A small pension plan with only $250 million in assets has different investment criteria than a very wealthy individual with a $10 million portfolio. Paradoxically, as implied above, the pension plan might be considered a small account for an institutional salesperson, while an individual investor with $10 million in the market would be considered a very large and important client for a retail broker.

Private client/retail brokerage

Inside the financial services industry, the term "private client group" is used more and more frequently to define the type of business handled by retail brokers. In the past, a private client group often referred to today's private wealth management divisions. In some companies, it still does. So it is important when looking at each firm to be clear about how they define each area. Generally, a private client group retail broker handles mutual fund purchases, relatively small stock and bond sales, and also works with the general investing public. Although retail brokers are not forbidden from working with very wealthy individuals, most of their clients are average upper middle-class workers who need advice about 401(k) rollovers, retirees living on fixed incomes and parents worried about saving money for their children's college education. These brokers handle day-to-day mutual fund purchases and relatively small stock and bond sales.

It's important to note that many who work in the private wealth management business worked in retail brokerage first. If you're considering a career in private wealth management, you should expect to spend time learning about the business as a retail broker at the beginning of your career. One way to look at the industry is to see private wealth management as a specialized ... of retail brokerage. At Merrill Lynch, for example, retail brokers can become private wealth managers as long as their average account size is $5 million or higher. Remember, a broker, for the most part, whether he or she works for retail, institutional or PWM is first a salesperson. More than anything else, the ability to sell determines how much success brokers have. A 24-year-old employee right out of business school might have a hard time at first convincing many wealthy clients to turn over their money to them. Like the private wealth management industry, retail brokerage is comprised of relationship-based selling that may have a transactional component, like the sale of an annuity to an investor. But brokers' success over the long term mainly relies upon their ability to earn their clients' trust in their impartial and, hopefully, profitable advice.

Institutional sales

Institutional sales brokers sell the primary research and investment opinions on companies covered by their firm to organizations like mutual funds, hedge funds and pensions, who will then buy stock in the companies covered if the research is favorable. For example, Raymond James and Associates is well known for research in oil services companies. Its institutional salespeople call upon mutual funds, etc., and share the firm's research about certain oil services companies. If the mutual fund companies like the research, they will buy stock in those companies based on the research from Raymond James. In turn, those stock purchases (and subsequent stock sales) generate commissions for the salespeople.

Institutional sales divisions do not handle private accounts of individuals. In rare instances, an institutional salesperson might have an account for a wealthy individual, but regular institutional clients are demanding and lucrative enough, so other types of accounts might not prove as profitable. In addition, the rules governing investment sales to institutions are different than those for sales to individual investors. The regulations assume that institutional clients, being professional investors, are more sophisticated than individuals. There is a lot less liability for recommendations in institutional sales than in retail, where brokers have to gauge not only their clients objectives, but also whether the clients are sophisticated enough to understand the implications of their investment strategies. Many institutional brokers choose not to deal with these liability issues.

Visit the Vault Finance Career Channel at **www.vault.com/finance** – with insider firm profiles, message boards, the Vault Finance Job Board and more.

VAULT CAREER LIBRARY

9

Private banking/private wealth

The main difference between a retail broker and a private wealth manager is account size. Most firms have minimum account sizes and production level requirements that salespeople must maintain to run their business through the private wealth management department. "Production" refers to the combination of fees and commissions generated by a salesperson. Because they are the largest producers of fees and commissions, private wealth managers often qualify for higher commission payment rates (called a higher payout) than regular retail brokers, and they benefit from a more intimate knowledge of the various departments offering services to wealthy clients because they work with these departments more often. Indeed, private wealth managers at the most prestigious Wall Street firms can command immense resources on behalf of a major multimillion-dollar (or billion-dollar!) client.

Private wealth managers maintain a higher degree of professional knowledge than most brokers. They not only need to know about investment instruments, but also taxation issues and estate planning. There are a number of products available only to accredited investors, like hedge funds, private equity and partnerships. These are rarely used by retail brokers because federal regulations make them available only to folks meeting certain net-worth and income thresholds.

Like those in the private client group, private wealth managers must rely on relationship selling in order to be successful. But instead of generating transaction commissions, private wealth managers generally charge management fees for handling a client's portfolio, which can range anywhere from 50 basis points (or 0.5 percent) of the value of a client's portfolio per year to 100 basis points (1 percent) or even higher in special circumstances.

Note that although in the above section we discussed retail brokers and institutional salespeople, as well as private wealth managers, this guide will focus exclusively on careers in private wealth management.

The History of Private Wealth Management

During the first 100 years or so after gaining its independence, the U.S. had a very small private banking system that provided most of the legal tender (money) in circulation at the time. Then a country of small-scale farming, the U.S. had many assets tied up in the value of its land, and there was a general prejudice against mortgages and debt of any sort, which represented a threat of land loss if not paid. Bankers who could repossess land were seen as suspicious characters. Attempts to foster a federally chartered bank became a campaign issue under President Andrew Jackson in 1829, who led a populist movement claiming that federal banking was illegal under the U.S. Constitution. The financial system fostered under such hostility was then made up of small, state-chartered banks that issued bank notes. Since these lacked liquidity, they were subject to various panics and bank failures, making banking a more risky proposition than it is today. Consequently, most investment was made in land, and this made sense, since the country's economy was largely agrarian, and land was unsettled and cheap.

It wasn't until the start of the Civil War in 1861 that the U.S. began to develop the rudiments of a modern banking system. Maintaining large modern armies required unprecedented amounts of money. The Union increasingly turned to modern methods of financing, including massive printing of paper money and issuing long-term debt with the help of financier Jay Cooke. Cooke sold over $1.3 billion in federal bonds to help finance the war, and his agents penetrated even the smallest towns across the country, selling not just an investment return from the bonds, but banking as a patriotic institution. Together with the National Banking Act of 1863, the bonds provided the basis for a national banking system and established a national currency.

The Gilded Age

The new banking system helped foster rapid industrial transformation in the U.S. during the latter half of the 19th century. With increased industrialization and liquidity came increased concentrations of paper money in individual hands, often known as wealth. Unlike land, handling paper wealth requires private wealth managers. With increasing confidence in the banking system, more and more wealthy people turned to professionals, who worked either for banks or for brokerage firms, helping clients invest and protect their capital.

Visit the Vault Finance Career Channel at **www.vault.com/finance** – with insider firm profiles, message boards, the Vault Finance Job Board and more.

VAULT CAREER LIBRARY   11

Ironically, a further boost to confidence in financial markets came in 1871 via the Great Chicago Fire. Though a number of insurance companies failed to pay clients in full, the largest and most notable firms from Hartford, Connecticut (the Hartford, Phoenix Mutual and Aetna) promptly paid all claims, allowing the city to rebuild with a better modern design than it had prior to the fire.

Additionally, in the later half of the 19th century, laws governing the creation of corporations were liberalized, making it easier to set these up and maintain them. As a result, wealth became more liquid and prevalent. The late 19th century and early 20th century saw unprecedented growth in the number of millionaires. Money, or paper wealth, became not just respectable, but admirable. This was the time of Horatio Alger and the strive-and-succeed stories that bred the hero-worship of industry captains like Cornelius Vanderbilt, John D. Rockefeller and Henry Huttleston Rogers. These men are now regarded as robber barons, because of their perceived rapacious business tactics and lack of ethical conduct.

The Great Depression and Reform

The central banking system of that time stayed in place with minor modifications (such as the Federal Reserve Act of 1913, which created the Federal Reserve) until the stock market crash in 1929. Many thought it resulted from speculative excesses by banks and brokerage firms that let clients without the proper means leverage their investments (borrow money to buy stock) beyond their capacity to repay. Others blamed easy credit terms that allowed consumers to fall deeper and deeper into debt.

This caused the federal government to enact legislation addressing various investment concerns. In 1932, the first of the Glass-Steagall Acts was passed, allowing the Federal Reserve to better control the money supply. A year later, the second half passed, separating the activities of brokerage firms and banks. The 1933 act also prohibited banks from owning brokerage firms, and spelled out in detail what specific financial data needed to be disclosed to investors when registering a new issue of securities. After, the Securities Act of 1934 was passed, regulating financial markets, such as stock and bond markets, and creating the Securities and Exchange Commission.

The end result, with respect to the wealth management industry, was that private banking or private wealth management remained fragmented. Banks, for instance, offered the types of services, like trusts and managed accounts, important to wealthy clients that brokerage firms didn't. Brokerage firms offered insurance products and management of individual stock purchases that banks couldn't. Because banks and brokerages didn't have competition for various types of business, they also lacked incentive to innovate, or provide imaginative solutions to clients' problems. This led to private wealth management, for many years, becoming a stodgy, stifling business.

The Roaring '90s

From 1990 through 1999, the Dow Jones Industrial Average rose from nearly 2,500 to over 11,000 points. With the markets growing at 34 percent each year (the S&P 500 has averaged about an 11 percent gain each year since 1970), even stodgy, naturally risk-adverse bankers began to calculate the profits they were missing out on by not participating in one of history's great bull runs. Accordingly, banks devised a number of strategies to circumvent Glass-Steagall to offer a full range of investment services. Lease agreements with specialized broker/dealers that only serviced banks became common, allowing the banks to lease brokerage employees. Instead of owning a brokerage they offered services through these leased employees. Brokerage firm investors realized that if banks could buy brokerage firms, said firms' share prices would rise because prices go up when there are more buyers. Brokerage firms would also benefit by gaining access to investors that previously only dealt in bank-issued and insured certificates of deposit.

Modifications were slowly made to the Act until 1999, when the Gramm-Leach-Bliley Financial Services Modernization Act repealed Glass-Steagall altogether, resulting in the modern financial services industry, which combines retail and commercial banking, insurance services and brokerage into one unit, with private wealth management departments serving the richest and often choicest private clients.

Visit the Vault Finance Career Channel at **www.vault.com/finance** – with
insider firm profiles, message boards, the Vault Finance Job Board and more.

VAULT CAREER LIBRARY

13

Private Wealth Management Employers and Clients

CHAPTER 2

The Players Today

With many of the old boundaries between banking, brokerage and insurance crumbling, today's financial services companies, whatever form they take, all must provide component products from each of the major industry areas. Banks offer insurance products, such as annuities and life insurance, while brokerage firms offer bank products, like checking accounts and mortgages, for example. This is especially true in private wealth management, where a variety of services from banking, brokerage and insurance can be marketed to the same client.

Banks

In the financial services industry, size still does matter. Consider this: the top three Wall Street investment firms' (Merrill Lynch, Goldman Sachs and Lehman Brothers) combined market capitalization is less than the market capitalization of Citigroup's alone. With muscle like that, banks like Citigroup have been able to buy up brokerage firms since 2000, although the rate has recently slowed. Of the money center banks, Citigroup, Bank of America, JPMorgan Chase, Wachovia, Bank of New York, SunTrust and Mellon rank among the largest that have active private wealth management divisions. Regional banks offering investment services through their own broker/dealer probably also have some type of private wealth management services, if only through their banks' trust departments. The quality of services and depth of knowledge may vary, however, amongst the smaller banks. Even savings and loans firms like Washington Mutual provide some trust and estate services, which are key components of private wealth management.

Banks sell a multitude of products, often providing captive or proprietary services for their clients, as well as general services. These are special product offerings packaged by the bank, and are only made available to clients of that bank. Such services might include a portfolio manager, who only manages money for clients of the bank. This has been a great advantage

Visit the Vault Finance Career Channel at **www.vault.com/finance** – with
insider firm profiles, message boards, the Vault Finance Job Board and more.

VAULT CAREER LIBRARY 15

for banks in that clients will be less likely to move to another firm, especially if they value the services of a portfolio manager doing a good job.

In general, of the various industry roles, banks pay the lowest commission rates to their private wealth managers, because many of their private wealth management clients may already be clients of the bank, doing business in other areas such as commercial banking or mortgages, and not because banks are stingy by nature. Clients may also do business with the bank because it has a good reputation and well-known name. A client might, for example, be persuaded that Bank of America is the place to do business because of the 692 commercials they see about it every day. The banks' ability to attract clients will greatly aid a private wealth manager. Though they might be paid lower commission rates, it doesn't mean they will make less money. The best private wealth managers tend to make about the same amount of money no matter which company they work for.

Wirehouse

"Wirehouse" is an industry term for a large national broker/dealer. Merrill Lynch, Goldman Sachs, Lehman Brothers and Bear Sterns are all examples of wirehouses that also provide private wealth management services. Wirehouses usually provide as many services as large money center banks when it comes to private wealth management. Like the banks, they also provide a number of proprietary or captive services, such as private portfolio managers and specialized private equity, which can boost client retention. Be warned, however, that proprietary services also have the drawback of not letting a private wealth manager move easily from one firm to another (with their clients, at least), hence the name captive services. Wirehouses also compensate managers on the lower end of the payout scale, but just like money center banks, they also attract more clients because of the perceived prestige of their names and reputations. Although this won't make finding clients easy, it might make it easier. A funny thing about money is that when clients turn a lot of it over to a manager, they want to know that the firm will still be there the next day. With a wirehouse, clients often get the comfort they seek from a known name.

The emphasis on investment is what differentiates wirehouses from banks, as they typically offer a broader array of investment options. Although this focus is disappearing as banks continue to buy brokerage firms, banks still tend to rely more on captive, in-house products than a broader set of investment products that you find in a wirehouse.

Regional and boutiques

Legg Mason, A.G. Edwards, Jefferies and Raymond James are all examples of regional firms that offer private wealth management services. Though not as well known outside the industry, these firms provide an array of products and services with a small firm focus on personal service. They also offer some proprietary or captive products, but generally allow their reps the freedom to sell products off their wholesale list without incentives to move proprietary products. Regional firms offer a slightly higher payout (approximately 10 to 15 percent higher) to wealth managers in most instances than banks or wirehouses, but working to land clients will be a little harder at a regional firm than at a better-known bank or brokerage firm.

Boutique firms are much smaller in size than the regionals and will usually have less than 100 reps. Not all boutiques will offer private wealth management services, and whether or not they do depends primarily on what types of products they emphasize. A small firm that specializes in smaller stocks will probably not have a very accomplished wealth management department.

Independents/insurance

A growing number of private wealth managers are choosing to open private practices with independent contractor and insurance company broker/dealers providing regulatory, product and compliance support. They also offer much higher payouts than the other types of firms—often twice as high. But these firms do not offer brick and mortar locations and other things like telephone systems, computers, etc. These necessities must be paid for out of the rep's own pocket. They also don't offer in-depth and in-house expertise in trusts, estates, tax and asset management like the regional firms, wirehouses and banks. However, private wealth managers working with an independent broker/dealer are free to hire their own experts and develop their own practice in a manner that best suits them and their clients. One caution: this is an option that should be reserved for only the most entrepreneurial of people. Especially at the beginning of your career, when the learning curve looks like

Visit the Vault Finance Career Channel at **www.vault.com/finance** – with insider firm profiles, message boards, the Vault Finance Job Board and more.

VAULT CAREER LIBRARY

17

the crux of a hockey stick, it's important to have the support of those who have experience in the business.

Wealth Management Clients

As previously mentioned, private wealth management clients come from varied backgrounds and walks of life. Generally, they can be divided into four separate groups: trusts, retirees, small business owners or professionals, and corporate executives. Each group has specific investment objectives and requirements.

Trusts, trust fund babies and "trustafarians"

In the case of trusts, the actual client is the trust, not the person who derives income or other distributions from it, known as the beneficiary. The types of investments that a private wealth manager can make on behalf of a trust are generally defined in writing within the trust documents, and the manager is governed by these limitations, not by the wishes of the beneficiary. The documents will also govern the distribution of income and principal from the trust.

Today, the phrase "trust fund baby" is still widely used to define those who live off of trust funds. Another term for trust fund baby is "trustafarian," which comes from the word rastafari and originated at the beginning of the 1990s to denote free-spirited kids living off of their parents' trust funds. Although the terms trust fund baby and trustafarian can be used interchangeably, trustafarian is considered a little more negative, as it's used to make fun of kids who don't have to face up to the responsibilities of working and paying bills. (Note that clients could be offended when referred to by either phrase.)

The Kennedy family probably includes America's best-known examples of trust fund babies. Paris Hilton is another type. Trust fund babies don't have to worry about saving the rainforest, and they don't have to be young. They only have to be under-employed and living off of an income that is substantially derived from a trust. Clients who have these and are gainfully employed to the extent that they do not have to live off of the income from the trust are not considered trust fund babies. This distinction is important because private wealth managers will manage money differently for those trust beneficiaries who are not relying greatly on their trusts for income. For these types of clients, growth of capital is going to be the most important investment objective, rather than protecting their money.

For trust fund baby clients, however, the most important services provided by private wealth managers are to: 1) protect the clients' wealth and 2) create income. Only after these two primary objectives are met can a wealth manager try to create additional wealth for the client. Rather than growing money, wealth managers generally put a higher premium on protecting it in the case of trust fund babies, because it is less likely that someone living off of a trust fund will find opportunities to create additional riches. Because trust fund babies don't have jobs in the traditional sense, or pursue wealth like corporate executives or small business owners, the money they have today is likely the only money that they will ever have. If the trust loses funds today, managers will have to make it back tomorrow at a higher rate of return to break even.

To illustrate this point, suppose Ellie has a trust portfolio of $10 million invested heavily in the technology-laden NASDAQ composite. This is a more risky strategy than investing in, say, big, blue-chip companies or corporate bonds. Say Ellie Mae's portfolio declines by 10 percent to $9 million in one year, then in order for her to get back to the original $10 million value, she'd have to make $1 million in the next year, or more than 11.1 percent. So in order to make up for a 10 percent loss, Ellie Mae would likely have to take more risk to make more than an 11.1 percent return.

Retirees

Although no legal document governs investment objectives for retirees, private wealth managers take into account the level of experience and the objectives of wealthy retired people when making investment recommendations. Often this will take the form of some sort of written questionnaire or summary stating the client's objectives and ability to take on risk. Very wealthy retired people share a number of the same problems with trust fund babies. They have the same concern with preserving wealth as do trusts, and are less likely to take risks in the market than other types of investors. Retirees also rely on their wealth to create income to live off of. But wealthy retirees have an additional challenge to meet that a private wealth manager can help with: how to structure their estate so as to leave it

Visit the Vault Finance Career Channel at **www.vault.com/finance** – with
insider firm profiles, message boards, the Vault Finance Job Board and more.

VAULT CAREER LIBRARY   19

to their heirs. Managers can help accomplish these goals using insurance products, trusts and other estate planning tools.

Small business owner or professionals

One of the most important client subsets for private wealth managers comes from small business owners having a private company or a professional private practice, like doctors, lawyers or even some private wealth managers. For many of these, much of their wealth is tied up in the value of their business. In addition to managing the client's liquid investments (stocks, bonds, etc.), a private wealth manager might also guide a small business owner or private practioner in selling their business—a unique type of transaction that even very sophisticated clients will often lack the requisite background to do with confidence. Private wealth management firms deal with companies, often specialized CPA firms, which evaluate the value of such businesses and facilitate the sale. In addition, private wealth managers might help with what is known as succession planning, a buyout of a company over a period of time by owners who will actively manage the business. These owners are often related either by birth or marriage to the previous owners. This type of arrangement would work with an older lawyer, for example, who has brought on a son as an associate.

Or, as another example, let's say Jane, after years of serving her boss and learning the private wealth management business, struck out on her own and convinced two clients, Ellie and Jethro, to move their accounts to a new firm where she was going to be a private wealth manager. Jane, using her natural sales skills, evident charisma and her deep appreciation for people, also attracted other clients over a period of years, and became a top salesperson for her private wealth management firm.

One of her best clients is a lawyer named Angela, with a thriving private practice. Angela's getting older and looking forward to spending less time in the office. She could either sell her business outright for cash, or she could bring in a junior partner who would then "succeed" her and gradually buy her out over a period of time. In either scenario, there are a number of questions that must be answered: How much is the business worth? Which is better, taking less cash now or more cash over a period of time? Will the business be worth more or less in the future? What are the tax implications in either scenario? How does this affect her heirs?

Jane can help with all of these questions by using the various departments within the private wealth management firm to get answers to each and design a plan that meets her clients' requirements.

Corporate executives

Rich corporate executives often become wealthy through stock and stock options in the company they work for. This type of wealth presents a number of challenges for clients, which can be effectively handled by private wealth managers.

Often, these stock or option agreements limit the amount of stock that can be sold or options that can be exercised at any given time. Imagine what would happen to a company if one of its top executives suddenly sold all of his or her stock. These clients are wealthy, but only on paper. They cannot readily turn their wealth into cash at any given moment. But through the use of derivates, such as synthetic options and other risk management strategies, private wealth managers can help protect the value of the executives' portfolio. In addition, some securities may be borrowed against under the proper circumstances so that the clients can derive some cash from these paper assets.

Let's look at another of Jane's clients: Clyde, a wealthy biotechnology executive for one of the top publicly traded molecular research companies. Clyde owns 53,000 shares of restricted stock in his employer, MegaGen of Chula Vista, Calif. Since last March, MegaGen has traded from $10 up to $73 based on a compound that was recently fast-tracked by the FDA. On paper, Clyde's stock is worth $3.8 million but he can't sell any of it for another 18 months because of the restriction placed on him by the company. He thinks the price will go up from here, but he realizes that having his wealth concentrated in one company is risky. But management also frowns on executives selling stock in the company because it may send a signal to shareholders and others that the executive thinks the price will go down. In the meantime, Clyde would like to get out of the starter home that he still lives in with his wife and two kids. But the down payment on the home he really wants would take every bit of cash he has, plus some he doesn't.

Jane has asked her firm's risk management department to take a look at MegaGen and devise an option strategy that can help minimize the market risk of Clyde's stock. Private wealth management firms can structure options

Visit the Vault Finance Career Channel at **www.vault.com/finance** – with insider firm profiles, message boards, the Vault Finance Job Board and more.

VAULT CAREER LIBRARY   21

on the stock to minimize the effect of price fluctuations. Based on the pledge of the stock as collateral (that is, pledging the value of the stock to cover a loan from the firm), Jane's firm is able to loan Clyde sufficient cash to cover the down payment for his new home.

Jane might also help with any complicated tax questions surrounding Clyde's stock and options. Since his estate is worth more than the maximum allowed to be transferred tax-free at death, and the sale of options or stock is subject to various taxes depending on how long they were owned, Jane must devise strategies with other members of her firm to minimize taxes. For example, Clyde might purchase insurance that would cover the amount of inheritance tax at his death. Or he might move the stock into a trust.

The super-rich

There are a handful of private wealth management clients out there for whom labels like "executive" or "professional" seem moot. Bill Gates is not just a software guy, after all. These are the super-rich, the ultra-high-net-worth clients, the ones who private wealth management firms court fiercely. They can be athletes, CEOs, movie stars, music moguls, oil barons—even royalty. And their needs are as diverse and unique as they are.

How does one manage the tax implications of a $10 million stock performance bonus? A seven-year, $85 million contract extension? An endorsement deal worth $50 million and sneakers for life? Maintenance for eight mansions and a fleet of classic cars? To generalize would be an exercise in futility.

However, there's one thing in common when it comes to these clients: private bankers are far more than just high-powered investment advisors. In some cases, they become de facto business managers, concierges and budgeters. For some clients, they not only invest money, but make sure that everyone in the family gets their allowance each month. For others, it's making sure that properties are well maintained and domestic staff is paid. And for still others, it's consulting on new contracts or deals and becoming intimately involved in the client's professional life—and even personal life.

For the private wealth manager, the firm's entire resource base—and even the large company's assets—are there to be used in serving these clients. When there are potentially billions in lifetime earnings at stake, no job is too small, large, obscure, inane or unusual. And the private bankers managing these

Investment Products

In addition to providing services to clients, private wealth managers also offer investment products that provide capital growth, income or both. And one class of investment products that we will cover, options, can be used to both provide income and manage risk.

Equity Investments

Common stock is the best known type of investment. Each share in a company, such as Starbucks, for example, represents a small percentage of ownership. The major advantage in owning common stock is that it can be bought or sold without difficulty, making it easy to convert ownership into cash. Also, as a stock's price grows, the increased value is tax-deferred until it is sold. The profit a client makes when the stock is sold is usually taxed at a lower rate than regular income. Another advantage is that investors do not have to actively manage anything, as they might if they owned other types of businesses like a chain of gas stations or stores, but can rely on professionals to manage their investments for them. One disadvantage is investors need to be very familiar with the company's operations to constantly gauge whether it is still a good investment.

Equity mutual funds are popular investment vehicles that allow average investors to hire professional money managers. Vanguard is one of the more popular mutual fund companies, and Vanguard U.S. Growth Fund Investor Shares (VWUSX), founded in 1959, is one its oldest funds. Vanguard pools investors' money and then a professional portfolio manager buys and sells common stock in various companies out of it to increase its value. The fund's value is determined by adding up all of the stock it owns at the close of business every trading day. That value is then divided by the number of shares outstanding to determine the share price or net asset value. One of the major advantages to shareholders in owning mutual funds is the professional investment management they get by using portfolio managers. They also get diversification of their assets. In addition, investors don't always have to make the buy and sell decisions in regard to the individual stocks they own. One disadvantage is that mutual funds' profits can be taxed at a higher rate than that of regular common stock. They also tend to require much more bookkeeping for tax purposes than other types of investments. Some critics feel that since mutual funds attract such large sums of money, over-diversification can be a problem.

Closed end investment companies, also known as closed end funds, are a cross between a mutual fund and common stock. A notable example of closed end fund is Berkshire Hathaway, run by legendary Wall Street wizard Warren Buffet. In short, Berkshire Hathaway's end product provides an investment return, just like Microsoft's end product is software. In Berkshire Hathaway, like a mutual fund, investors gather their money into a pool that is then managed by Warren Buffet. Unlike a mutual fund, however, a closed end investment company trades independently of its actual asset value and might end the day with a net asset value of $9 but a share price of $9.50. A mutual fund must sell for its net asset value, but a closed end fund's share price is determined by whatever price investors pay for it on a trading market, just like IBM's or Chevron's share price. Closed end companies will often invest in specific industries, such as banking or software, or in specific geographical areas like developing countries or Eastern Europe.

Closed end investment companies tend to be a little more tax efficient and smaller in size than mutual funds, thus easier to manage. Clients pay a regular stock commission to buy these funds, plus a fee to the managers. These expenses are usually higher than those charged by mutual funds.

Unit investment trusts (UITs), are simple investments in either stocks or bonds, easily recognizable to clients. However, they are generally not as tax-friendly as common stock or even mutual funds. Like mutual funds and closed end funds, these trusts pool investor money. However, UITs use "passive management" of a fixed portfolio of assets or stock, meaning no additional buying and selling in the portfolio. For example, Dow Theory (often referred to as Dogs of the Dow) states that if you buy the 10 highest dividend-yielding stocks in the Dow Jones Industrial Average in January and hold them for one year, you will outperform the market. The theory works modestly well, and because it relies on buying stock in companies well known by the average investor and using a passive investment strategy, Wall Street insiders recognized that if they packaged the strategy inside a UIT they'd have a product popular with investors. UITs are meant to be held until a fixed expiration date, at which point the net asset value is returned to the investor. Although some companies allow investors to sell at the net asset value earlier than the expiration date, every UIT is different and some may need to be held until the expiration date of the underlying trust.

Fixed Income Investments

Preferred stock is a type of equity with superior rights over common stock in a company. Often, one of these rights is a dividend, which is a fixed percentage of the preferred stock's par value (the original value for which the stock was issued). For example, GM may have a preferred stock that pays a 5 percent dividend on a $25 par value, meaning it pays 5 percent of $25. When a preferred issue has dividends attached to it, the company distributes these to preferred shareholders before giving any to common stockholders. The rights to these dividends may expire in one year's time or be cumulative over a period of time. In addition, preferred shareholders have superior claim over common shareholders to the assets of the company in case of liquidation. Preferred shares might also be convertible (known as convertible preferred stock) into shares of common stock in lieu of dividend payments. Dividends are generally paid on a quarterly basis. Because the cash flow created by preferred stock is often attractive to investors looking for income, and preferred stock offers some opportunity for growth, it can be a good option for conservative clients looking for maximum cash return and modest growth. The downside for investors is that dividends are taxed as ordinary income, and the growth potential is often negligible.

Bonds are notes issued in $1,000 increments (called the par value or principal) that pay a stated rate of interest (called the coupon rate) and require the debtor to return the principal, or par value, back to the investor at a specified time (called maturity). Generally, bonds are issued for periods of one, two, five, 10, 20 and 30 years. Longer periods carry higher interest rates than shorter periods. As prevailing interest rates go up or down, bonds trade for either more or less than their par value to reflect the going market interest rates. Let's say that 30-year corporate interest rates are now 5 percent. A corporate bond that was issued last year that carried a coupon rate of 4.8 percent would now trade at 96 (that is, 96 percent of par value) or $960. Interest rates and bond values have an inverse relationship. As interest rates go up, bond values go down. As interest rates go down, bond values go up. Bonds may be callable—meaning the issuer can "call" it back and give an investor back his or her principal—after a period of time as well. Thus, if

Visit the Vault Finance Career Channel at **www.vault.com/finance** – with insider firm profiles, message boards, the Vault Finance Job Board and more.

VAULT CAREER LIBRARY   25

interest rates go down too much, the issuer will call the bonds back, returning the par value to investors because they can issue other bonds to replace these at lower interest rates. Bonds may be backed by specific assets or revenue, or may be completely unsecured. They may be convertible to shares of common stock as well. Bonds are often used in loans to secure real estate purchases since the value of the land can secure investors' money. The three types of major bonds are corporate, treasury and municipal, and each carries different risk factors with different tax rates.

Corporate bonds provide the highest rate of interest out of the three major classes. They also hold the most risk. Interest rates for bonds are determined by the length to maturity (when the investor will get his money back), the assets or lack thereof that back up the bonds and the credit rating of the offering company. Several firms, such as Standards & Poor's and Fitch Ratings, analyze the creditworthiness of issuing companies and provide ratings that grade bonds' quality on the investors' expectation of getting their money back. These ratings vary from high-quality investment grade bonds (most likely to get their money back), to lesser bonds called junk bonds (less likely to get their money back), to distressed bonds (fat chance of getting any money back) that are in default on payments to investors.

Corporate bonds are generally taxed at a higher rate than other types, which means that corporations must offer higher interest rates so investors retain the same amount of money after paying taxes as they would if they had invested in lower taxed bonds. The amount of money kept after paying taxes is called the after-tax yield.

Advantages provided by corporate bonds include relatively high interest rates, the availability of investment-grade bonds, regular interest payments and investing ease. The downside for bond buyers is that inflation may eat away at after-tax yield. Also, interest rates could go up, and investors would then be stuck with bonds that pay less than the going rate. Another concern is that if interest rates go down, the issuer may call back the bonds, forcing investors to invest at the prevailing lower interest rates.

Treasury bonds are issued by the federal government and are often considered one of the safest investments. After all, to pay off the bonds, the government only needs to raise taxes. Because Treasuries are backed by the full faith and credit of the U.S. (as well as its taxing power), they enjoy unrivaled prestige in world finance today.

Treasuries are issued in three-month, six-month, two-year, three-year, five-year, 10-year and 30-year maturities. Economists and Wall Street types look at the differences in interest rates in the range of maturities in Treasury bonds to get an idea of where the economy is headed. This range is called the spread. A tighter or smaller spread, it is often claimed, can forecast uncertain economic activity. Because Treasuries are not considered as risky, they have lower interest rates than other types of bonds. However, Treasuries are subject to the two types of risk discussed previously: inflation, and the possibility that interest rates will go up.

Municipal bonds are issued by cities, states, counties and other non-federal government entities. In accordance with United States Supreme Court ruling, municipal bonds, or munis, are free from federal taxation in most cases. Also, municipal bonds may not be subject to state taxes, although regulations vary from state to state. Since municipalities can offer investors the same after-tax yields at lower interest rates as other issuers, bonds are a major advantage for said municipalities, in that they are a less expensive method for raising money. Some types of munis include: general obligation bonds, containing the promise to pay by the municipality as a general obligation; revenue bonds, backed by specific taxes or fees, like money collected on a toll road; and hospital bonds, used to finance the building of public hospitals.

The same agencies that rate corporate bonds on a company's likelihood to pay also rate munis. Municipalities that exercise responsible fiscal management enjoy a higher rating, and are able to borrow money at lower rates than those not as responsible. Because municipalities can rely upon tax revenue to repay investors, like the federal government does, munis are generally considered somewhat less risky than corporate bonds, depending on the issue. However, municipal bonds are also subject to the same two types of risk previously discussed in relation to bonds:inflation, and the possibility that interest rates will go up.

Bond mutual funds function just like equity mutual funds, but invest in bonds and pass along interest payments to their investors. The benefit to investors is in having professionals manage a diversified portfolio of bonds. The disadvantage is that bond funds are not as tax efficient. Bonds are generally not meant to be bought and sold but are often included in a fund. This means that capital gains are passed along to investors, who then have to pay taxes on the gains. Also, investors don't benefit from a maturity date at which time their principal will be retuned, which they would if they owned

Visit the Vault Finance Career Channel at **www.vault.com/finance** – with insider firm profiles, message boards, the Vault Finance Job Board and more.

VAULT CAREER LIBRARY   **27**

individual bonds. Lastly, a portfolio of individual bonds does not charge investors a management fee, which reduces the amount of return, as a bond fund does.

Closed end bond funds are also very similar to their equity brother, the closed end investment company, except that they invest in, yes, bonds. Again, these funds don't promise to return principal, like a single bond would, although investors do receive professional management.

Real estate investment trusts (REITs) are investment companies that invest in real estate properties and mortgages. Under IRS regulations, REITs are required to pass along 90 percent of their taxable income to their investors. Accordingly, REITs often pay higher income yields than bonds, and when real estate markets rise, the share prices of REITs also tend to go up. On the downside, real estate markets can be hard to predict, and are sometimes forecast on interest rates and other general economic factors that make them a challenge to manage, even for experienced real estate managers. And when real estate markets are bad, they often stay that way for longer periods of time than other parts of the economy.

Products Requiring Accreditation

These products can only be sold to clients meeting certain income or net worth criteria. According to the Securities and Exchange Commission, these include individuals with a net worth in excess of $1 million; a person with income in each of the last two years of at least $200,000 ($300,000 when combined with a spouse); and a trust with assets topping $5 million.

Hedge funds are becoming an increasingly popular investment alternative for the wealthy because they can take advantage of investment techniques not always available to mutual funds and other portfolio managers, like short sales that can lower the amount of risk for investment portfolios. This is especially important during periods of volatility, such as what we have experienced over the past few years. A short sale occurs when an investor borrows stock and sells it in the open market, anticipating that the price will go down and he or she will be able to buy it back at a lower price. Using this technique, hedge fund managers are able to make money for clients regardless of the overall direction of the stock market. If the market goes up, clients make money; if the market goes down, clients make money. (That is, if the hedge fund manager is good.)

One of the concerns in the hedge fund industry, however, is the lack of regulation, which could hurt investor confidence if more people with less experience are drawn to the industry just because it happens to be hot. Another drawback is the relative lack of liquidity. Unlike mutual funds, which require investors to liquidate their shares at the end of the business day when requested, hedge funds can take as long as 30 days to liquidate investor holdings.

Private equity funds invest in companies in anticipation of taking them public. A private equity firm will often have an investment banking department that will provide investors with the opportunity to invest in companies prior to going public. Because, at this stage, companies are generally rising in value, this can prove to a very good strategy for investors. However, these investments are generally illiquid, require a time horizon of more than two years and contain a degree of risk and sophistication not found in the common wealthy investor.

Private portfolio management involves wealthy clients having portfolio managers to actively manage their investments in the same manner as a mutual fund manager, but instead of owning shares in the fund, the clients own a regular portfolio of common stock. This strategy is more tax efficient than others, and provides a degree of diversification. Often, clients enjoy the personal service they receive in this arrangement, though it is a little more expensive than some other strategies.

Decrease your T/NJ Ratio
(Time to New Job)

Use the Internet's most targeted job search tools for finance professionals.

Vault Finance Job Board

The most comprehensive and convenient job board for finance professionals. Target your search by area of finance, function, and experience level, and find the job openings that you want. No surfing required.

VaultMatch Resume Database

Vault takes match-making to the next level: post your resume and customize your search by area of finance, experience and more. We'll match job listings with your interests and criteria and e-mail them directly to your inbox.

VAULT
> the most trusted name in career information™

Positions and Job Responsibilities

CHAPTER 4

Positions at Private Wealth Management Firms

The pivotal role in private wealth management is the private banker. This is the person who evaluates a client's financial position, recommends solid investments, and helps with the fiduciary aspects of their client's accounts (regularly consulting tax and accounting experts within the firm). The private banker can even set up a family office for wealthier clients to pay bills, staff and make sure family members are appropriately taken care of, or "given their allowances" as one banker put it.

Analysts

The career track for the private banker is fairly cut-and-dry at the major corporate banks and Wall Street brokerage firms. Undergrads coming in are called analysts, just as they are in sales and trading, corporate finance and everywhere else within the corporation. They're the ones who do all the researching, number crunching, report writing and, yes, coffee fetching on occasion, for the higher-ups who are actually working for the clients.

Being an analyst at a private bank is very much akin to similar roles in trading and investment banking. If a private banker needs an analysis done on a client's tax status, you'll tap the appropriate expertise within the firm to draw up the report. If a client is looking for a hedge fund investment with a specific strategy, you'll provide the banker or relationship manager with the best options. And while the banker can be called at any time to address a client's needs, you'll be called by the banker to assist and probably will keep longer hours on top of that as well.

The rewards can be fairly standard for the financial industry, with starting salaries ranging around $45,000 to $60,000 annually. Bonuses can be lighter than those given to investment bankers, however, and in the $15,000 to $30,000 range. At smaller firms, that bonus range can vary from analyst to analyst, depending on how useful they were in addressing client needs. The

Visit the Vault Finance Career Channel at **www.vault.com/finance** – with insider firm profiles, message boards, the Vault Finance Job Board and more.

VAULT CAREER LIBRARY   31

same goes for larger firms, of course, but the range is smaller, especially if there's an entire analyst class to consider.

Associates

The next rank up is associate, or just plain old private banker at the smaller firms. These are the guys who work with the clients and attract new business, the real face of the private bank for most clients. This is considered a very entrepreneurial job, in that you'll be expected to not only serve clients, but attract new clients as well. At many firms, you'll also be expected to attempt to sell your clients on the company's proprietary financial products, though the practice is starting to be curtailed at some firms.

Associates work closely with clients to create an overall financial strategy that encompasses not only investment, but income management, budget, real estate holdings, taxes, small business partnerships, estate planning and even paying the day-to-day bills of the household, all depending on the level of service the client wants (and the fees he or she is willing to pay, but at this level, fees are a secondary consideration to impeccable service and peace of mind).

Associate pay generally mirrors other Wall Street positions, with a newly minted associate making about $95,000 per year. Bonuses can vary, however, depending on how the firm structures compensation. Some private bankers receive bonuses solely on selling the client new services and the company's investment products, getting a percentage of the business the private bank brings in from that client. Others have more complex metrics, measuring performance against the client's stated goals. For example, some private wealth management clients may not want anything more complex than safe fixed-income investments that generate income with little or no risk, of 5 percent yield each year. If the private banker reached that goal, he would get a larger bonus than he would have if the investment only yielded 4.85 percent.

Some private wealth management firms eschew commission bonuses altogether, preferring to grant bonuses that do not give clients the appearance that their banker is simply interested in selling them products. These firms' bonus metrics are primarily based on fulfilling the clients' goals—a few firms even ask clients to review their bankers each year. Of course, firms will always appreciate it when associates convince their clients to use the private bank's estate planning services instead of someone else's, and in that sense, selling a non-investment service is seen as very bonus-worthy.

Likewise, associates are expected to drum up new business, and bonuses can come if you manage to gain new clients. Sometimes this will come from word-of-mouth, as current clients recommend the associate to their high-net-worth peers. It also comes from good old-fashioned networking, which means an investment on the associate's part in both time and, occasionally, money—especially when belonging to the right club or attending the right charitable event can mean a room full of potential clients. Some private banking firms organize cultural events or sports outings for their clients as well, with the hopes that they'll bring well-moneyed colleagues or friends for associates to network with.

Vice presidents

In time, salaries and bonus money for motivated, skilled and trusted associates can top $500,000, usually anywhere from five to eight years, depending on the firm and opportunities that have presented themselves, and up to $1 million within 10 to 13 years of private banking. At that level, however, an associate has often already been promoted to vice president. As such, he or she can be placed in a position overseeing a number of associates, or even a regional office. Alternatively, an associate that has specialized in spotting unique investment opportunities or has helped come up with new products can branch off from the client business and into an investment specialty. They may end up as market strategists or in-house portfolio consultants, gaining a smaller piece of individual clients' business, but making up for it by consulting with larger numbers of clients. Note, though, that VPs do not necessarily have to become specialists or managers, and can simply be super-producers.

Managing directors

Finally, after years of service—and income that can top $2 million or more for the best performing vice presidents—a successful, entrepreneurial, client-driven VP can be named a managing director. (Again, they may also remain super-producers, focusing only on their own super-high-net-worth clients.) In these positions, an MD can expect to be in charge of associates in a major branch office, or even in a firm's headquarters. They can be given the

Visit the Vault Finance Career Channel at **www.vault.com/finance** – with insider firm profiles, message boards, the Vault Finance Job Board and more.

VAULT CAREER LIBRARY

33

highest-net-worth clients, or the problem clients whose money is just too valuable for the firm to lose. In specialty positions, they may end up as the private bank's chief investment officer, chief fiduciary officer or general counsel. There are generally only a handful of MDs within any private wealth management firm, and they are often on the executive committees of the firm. At this level, salaries enter a realm in which the MD may want to find a private banker of his own, and are generally high enough that firms don't discuss them, though still nowhere near the level where they have to be reported to the Securities and Exchange Commission!

How Do Private Wealth Managers Work Within Their Firms?

By now, you might have guessed that private wealth management business is fairly complex. Take heart. Though private wealth managers need to understand all of the wealth management tools available to them, it's not as daunting as it may seem. Managers are not expected to master each area's details. Rather, they should be able to work with various specialists at their firm to find solutions most appropriate for their clients. Jane, in the previous example, by listening to Clyde's concerns and understanding his situation, was able to approach a department inside her firm to fashion a solution solving Clyde's problem.

The field is constantly changing. New tax regulations or rules governing trusts and insurance or new products are continually updated. One of the great challenges for managers is staying abreast of new products and services offered by their firms. They must then learn how they can practically apply them in real-life situations. Although your firm will provide you with plenty of opportunity to learn, the key will be how receptive you are to continue to practice and learn the trade. As the point person in your firm's relationship with clients, your ability to listen to your clients and work with the various experts in your firm to find solutions to their financial problems is the most important asset the firm has in maintaining a strong client relationship.

Job Responsibilities

Now let's look at what private wealth managers do on a daily basis.

Sales

Do wealth managers need to be good at Sales? Marketing? Investing? Schmoozing?

The answer to all of these questions is yes. A private wealth manager must be good at many things, including sales and prospecting for sales.

If your heart fell a little when you read that you'd have to, gasp, gulp … s … s … sell, then hold on for just a minute. The first stop on the road to success for any private wealth manager (or any other salesperson or manager for that matter) is to improve his or her listening skills. A good private wealth manager will be able to draw out a client's needs by asking the right questions then actively listening to the answers for cues and clues as to what the client might be thinking.

Money can be a very uncomfortable subject for people. Studies have shown that many people are more uncomfortable talking about money then they are about being naked in front of a strange doctor. Like a doctor, a private wealth manager's bedside manner, so to speak, will go a long way to identifying a client's needs.

When you improve your listening skills, you will find that you become a true professional salesperson. Such a professional salesperson is not someone who can simply talk another person into anything. A professional salesperson, rather, is an expert at listening to what clients need and filling that need by identifying a product or service appropriate for them. This means that often you are not selling anyone anything at all. Rather, you are listening to clients, building relationships with them, and understanding what their goals are. That's what sales is really all about. If you let it, it can be one of the best parts of your job.

Marketing

Marketing is the art of telling people who you are—whether you're a product or service—and why people should want to do business with you. This last part (why people should want to do business with you) is the most important

Visit the Vault Finance Career Channel at **www.vault.com/finance** – with
insider firm profiles, message boards, the Vault Finance Job Board and more.

VAULT CAREER LIBRARY   **35**

aspect of promoting your business. And since private wealth management is a highly-regulated industry, there are some notable challenges to marketing.

When it comes to marketing itself, the private wealth management industry has more restrictions on what it can lawfully claim than some other industries. For example, if you had owned an oil company and sold gasoline, like Jed Clampett, you could say that your gasoline made cars more fun to drive to promote your particular brand of gasoline. In the private wealth management business, though, it's a little more difficult to make claims of being "the best," or being "better than" something or someone else. Generally, the marketing is pretty standard, with some notable exceptions. Private wealth management companies might say they offer some sort of superior service quality or a degree of caring that may be missing from a competing firm. For instance, Raymond James and Associates offers BIO (by invitation only) visits to clients meeting certain liquid net-worth thresholds. These potential clients are flown down to Raymond James corporate headquarters and given a tour of the firm's four-acre campus in St. Petersburg, Florida. Clients then can meet with various departments of the firm, including the senior management, right up to the CEO.

What some firms lack in old-fashioned marketing, they allow (and expect) you to make up for. Some wealth managers may use newsletters to promote themselves, others network in their community. How you market yourself will be a decision to make after thoroughly evaluating what strengths you can bring to your clients.

Many managers spend time on the golf course to meet prospective clients. But golfing isn't a marketing strategy that can replace the hard work of meeting or calling prospects. It might be one component of a networking plan, which may also include volunteering on community boards, doing charity work and getting involved in other activities that allow a wealth manager to have more contact with wealthy individuals.

Investing

Private management firms provide their wealth managers with professionals to help them handle their clients' day-to-day investment decisions. This does not mean that wealth managers won't have a lot of input about those decisions or that they could not make those types of decisions themselves given the time. But think for a moment about how their time should be best spent?

Talking to clients? Prospecting for new clients? Meeting new contacts? Learning about new estate planning techniques? Or keeping a close eye on the market?

Certainly they need to develop well-informed opinions about investing and various investment strategies. And the most important function of a wealth manager in the investment process will be explaining the implications of the various strategies presented, thereby helping his or her clients select the most appropriate strategy.

The Rules and Regulations

As stated earlier, the private wealth management industry is governed by many rules and regulations. Managers must be thoroughly familiar with these, since they use them every day. These rules serve to protect investors from unscrupulous sales practices, regulating markets for buying and selling investments, like stocks and bonds, and generally instilling confidence in financial markets in the U.S.

Private wealth managers must first pass several licensing requirements before working with members of the public. This ensures that all of them have a minimum familiarity with the rules and regulations governing securities transactions. Managers need a Series 7 general securities license and, in most cases, a Series 63 state license. You can obtain them through your firm, which should be able to supply study materials and pay for you to sit for the examination.

A word of caution: the Series 7 and 63 exams are not impossibly difficult, but you need to study through a reputable service that provides exam prep materials in order to pass.

Visit the Vault Finance Career Channel at **www.vault.com/finance** – with
insider firm profiles, message boards, the Vault Finance Job Board and more.

VAULT CAREER LIBRARY   37

GETTING HIRED

Hiring Basics

CHAPTER 5

What it Takes

Compassion is key

What's the single biggest asset you can have if you want to pursue a career in private wealth management? Accounting? Investing savvy? Tax knowledge?

Try compassion, perhaps one of the rarest qualities to be found on Wall Street.

There's far more to private wealth management than numbers, and the single biggest preconception that newcomers bring into the field is that the numbers are paramount. Clients want someone who not only understands their finances, but truly understands their reasoning for doing what they want to do with their money.

"You really need good interpersonal skills and the ability to connect with people," says Isabel Sloan, global head of human resources for JPMorgan Private Bank, the private wealth management arm of JPMorgan Chase & Co. "It's the ability to make them feel comfortable discussing things that they'd otherwise feel uncomfortable talking about."

Certainly, many high-net-worth individuals view their private banker as simply another employee, or a valued consultant. But after a while, many private bankers say some clients practically adopt them into their families.

"I've helped one of my clients through two divorces, three marriages, prenups, divorce, home buying and selling, the whole thing," says one private banker. "They end up turning to you in the happiest times and in the god-awful worst times imaginable, and you really have to step up and be there, not only with the financial part, but with the personal part, too."

So first and foremost, there has to be a willingness to do whatever you can for the client. Part and parcel with that is the understanding that some clients may not want an intimate level of service, and you must have the judgment to determine those personal preferences as well.

The rest, many bankers say, can be taught. And in many ways that's reassuring for those who don't have a high finance background. The profit-at-any-cost approach commonly found on Wall Street isn't necessarily

Visit the Vault Finance Career Channel at **www.vault.com/finance** – with insider firm profiles, message boards, the Vault Finance Job Board and more.

VAULT CAREER LIBRARY   41

welcome at most firms. That said, driven and ambitious personalities are still welcome, so long as you can focus that ambition on fulfilling your clients' needs to the best of your ability and use your drive to attract new clients to the company.

Analytics help, but it's still personal

For those possessing more of a mathematical or analytical bent, your nature and the skills it engenders can certainly help you—and your clients—do very well. However, unlike a lot of activities on Wall Street, private wealth management can't be systemized. You may have tried and true systems for building an extensive and successful fixed-income portfolio, for example, but your client may simply want to go in another direction, leaving you to pound your head on your desk, baffled by the illogic of it all.

"This is one of the most personality-driven businesses you'll ever be in," said the chief investment officer of a mid-size private wealth management firm. "All the technical brilliance you possess won't matter one bit if you can't relate to the client."

That said, you still need to be driven and rather "type A" to succeed in private wealth management. A laid-back demeanor may certainly help relax clients to a point, but you better have thought out every option you've presented to them and have a few alternatives for each as well. Private bankers do a lot of "what if" projections, trying to plan for every contingency in their client's lives. That calls for a proactive mindset and a lot of self-direction. Waiting for your client to give you something to do is the surest way to lose a client.

But in the end, you have to care about your client. In most cases, these individuals worked hard for their money, or it's a family legacy passed down to them. It's an awesome responsibility, and the personality that can not only accept that, but see it as a positive challenge, will have a long career in private wealth management.

Many private wealth management firms, while stressing compassion and ethics, still remain very fee driven, with private bankers paid in direct proportion to the business they bring in and the money they make for their clients.

A few firms have begun implementing more team-like approaches, with multiple people dedicated to the same clients. These teams involve not only a private banker, but also tax managers, estate planners, planned giving advisors, legal counsel and even art appraisers, all wrangled together by a "relationship manager," a kind of concierge that brings the client all these experts as needed.

Educational Requirements

At the biggest firms, those tied to a major money-center bank or Wall Street brokerage, there are generally two entry-level positions, one for recent college graduates and the other for those who have completed their MBA.

Recent college graduates

Most private wealth management firms aren't too concerned about your undergraduate degree. Anywhere from a quarter to a third of the new hires fresh out of college do not have a business or business-related degree. That doesn't necessarily mean a degree in comparative religion is going to help you per se, but it might not be a drawback, either. Business and economics majors will generally have a leg up, but liberal arts students may also attract positive attention. However, a quantitative background, or even hard science work, won't necessarily give you an edge, since private banking is considered more of a relationship-focused career choice than many others on Wall Street.

For business or economics majors, you should even out your transcript with some liberal arts classes, particularly in psychology and sociology. Liberal arts majors should at least have a smattering of business and economics classes as well. A hard sciences major should focus more on business and at least one social science. As with most other after-college jobs these days, internships, extracurricular activities and any other evidence of self-motivation will help immensely. Service-oriented activities and philanthropic projects can be just as important as the school's investment club presidency.

Those applicants who do not have an MBA will likely be hired at the lowest rung on the private wealth management ladder, where they'll be given intensive training and on-the-job exposure to the detail work that will help them gain a deep understanding of the work the private bank does. It can take two to three years of this kind of work at a major private bank before this type of hire is given regular clients.

Visit the Vault Finance Career Channel at **www.vault.com/finance** – with insider firm profiles, message boards, the Vault Finance Job Board and more.

V∧ULT CAREER LIBRARY

43

Given that private wealth management is certainly not an undergraduate major, or minor, or even focus, recruiters generally look at students from a variety of schools. Students and recent grads hailing from the top undergraduate business schools—Pennsylvania's Wharton, MIT's Sloan, the University of Virginia's McIntyre school, Emory's Goizueta school or Notre Dame's Mendoza school—will raise eyebrows and catch notice, as will your high-end Ivy League and other notable private and public schools. Going to school in a major financial center such as New York, Chicago or San Francisco helps, too. However, at this level, solid coursework, a strong GPA and a compelling cover letter or recruiting interview will do far more for you than mediocrity distilled into a nice piece of paper from a prestigious school.

Graduate school and the MBA

Alternatively, those who went on to graduate school before settling on a career in private wealth management can find entry at the associate level, where, after training for anywhere from two to six months, they can begin working with clients.

Other private wealth management firms, usually the ones not attached to multibillion-dollar banking and investment corporations, tend to hire more experienced people. Someone fresh out of college may be given a shot at a low-level position, but they are generally the exception. Undergraduates with a few years' experience in the financial industry, in sales and trading generally, can catch on more easily at the smaller firms. (And bear in mind that smaller doesn't always equate to less prestigious.) MBA holders can likewise take up a starting position, sometimes with immediate client contact, right after grad school.

Specialization in investment and wealth management is, of course, a top priority for a would-be private banker's MBA program. While corporate accounting and management classes could be helpful in choosing a good investment, a future private wealth manager should focus on portfolio theory, wealth building and courses in interpersonal relationships and ethics in business school.

Certainly, the top-ranked MBA programs—Northwestern, Stanford, University of Chicago, Harvard, University of Pennsylvania, etc.—are at or near the top of any private wealth management recruiter's list, and a look at *BusinessWeek*'s or *U.S. News & World Report*'s annual rankings can give you an idea of the most well-regarded schools. Programs that offer concentrations in portfolio management, such as Baruch College in New York, MIT's Sloan School or UCLA's Anderson School, also produce sought-after MBA graduates. Some expanding private wealth management firms also look for an international background, which makes MBAs from Georgetown University or George Washington University in Washington D.C., an interesting option if you want to head overseas.

The aforementioned educational qualifications are for general private banking duties. Those who wish to work for a private wealth management company in a more specialized role will need the appropriate educational background. For example, undergraduate and graduate degrees in accounting, or even a law degree with a tax law concentration, would help with a tax specialty, while concentrations in real estate in either business school or law school could make you an expert attractive not only to a private bank, but a wide variety of other businesses. There are even graduate degrees available in philanthropic studies and nonprofit management (most notably at the University of Indiana's Center on Philanthropy) for those wanting to help the high-net-worth client make a difference. These specialized positions aren't entry-level jobs, and could be intriguing post-graduate jobs within private wealth management, though typically only at the largest firms.

Internships

In wealth management, internships are primarily offered to business school students between the first and second years of their MBA programs. Also, as with most industries, larger firms tend to have the structured internship programs for undergraduates as well.

These internships, such as the ones offered by Morgan Stanley, UBS, Goldman Sachs and JPMorgan, give a would-be private banker an inside look at how these institutions work. The internships are often very structured, with most of the time spent in classroom-like settings, or going around to different departments within the firm to discuss the firm's inner workings. Depending on the institution, interns are then sent to work with a private banker or a client team for the last few weeks of their eight to 12 week experience.

Visit the Vault Finance Career Channel at **www.vault.com/finance** – with insider firm profiles, message boards, the Vault Finance Job Board and more.

VAULT CAREER LIBRARY   **45**

MBA

Some interns find the experience exceptionally informative, but many others chafe at the lack of hands-on work. Bear in mind, however, that interns are often targeted for recruitment after they receive their MBA.

Smaller firms also offer internships—new opportunities with Washington Mutual's new wealth management arm and internships with Bingham Legg Advisers LLC are just a couple—and these can be far more intellectually stimulating. These firms actually put their interns to work far more quickly than the big companies, and the real world experience can be very energizing and educational. It can also be draining, however, as your supervisors may have no compunction about using you and your educational experience for all you're worth, even if it means 12-hour days during your summer break.

Both small and large private wealth management firms will take note of particularly successful interns, and can make positions available once you receive your MBA. And there's no barrier to going to work for a firm different than the one for which you interned.

Undergraduate

Many larger diversified financial companies offer undergraduate internships directly with the private bank, and some can put you not only in New York, but also in satellite offices around the country, where you'll see a better ground-level view of the business. These five- to eight-week programs serve as kind of an introduction to private banking, and are useful for the private bank to analyze potential candidates for entry-level positions the following spring. Undergrads will find the exposure a key experience in whether to go into private banking or not, as the internships are structured to give them as much information as possible (within a short timeframe) about the workings of the firm.

Licensing

There aren't as many licensing issues in private wealth management as there can be in other Wall Street professions. Private bankers are usually required to obtain their Series 7 and Series 63 or 66 certifications from the National Association of Securities Dealers (NASD), the self-regulatory arm of the investment industry.

The Series 7, or General Securities Representative certification, allows you to buy or sell, or solicit the purchase or sale, of all securities products, including corporate securities, municipal securities, municipal fund securities, options, direct participation programs, investment company products and variable contracts. It's the most basic form of certification for anybody involved with the markets, and is generally expected of anyone applying for a job at a PWM firm.

The majority of firms will also require a Series 63 certification, which requires knowledge of state securities laws and allows you to be a securities agent. Other firms may require the Series 66, which covers the same ground as a Series 63, but also certifies you to act as a registered investment adviser.

If you're fresh out of undergrad or business school and have entered into an associate program, your firm will nearly always sponsor your Series 7 and 63 exams, and any other exams they deem necessary, paying your test fees along the way. The Series 7 costs $250, while the Series 63 is another $82 and the Series 66 is $113. Most financial firms will pick up these costs for entry-level candidates—be wary of the ones that advertise entry-level positions, but won't pick up the tab for these tests. Higher level jobs at PWM firms come with the assumption that you already have the appropriate certifications, so make sure your paperwork is in order and everything's up to date before applying.

The Hiring Process

As with most Wall Street jobs, private wealth management firms are aggressive on-campus recruiters. At the undergraduate level, this takes place during the first semester of the school year, with recruiters conducting interviews right on campus for full-time and summer intern positions. The second round of interviews, if the student is selected for one, usually occurs soon afterward, and happens at the firm's home office.

If your school doesn't customarily receive recruitment visits from financial companies, you should be prepared to start sending in resumes for full-time employment early in the first semester of your senior year, if not earlier. Recruiters target certain schools because they've had success there before— so getting out in front of the human resources department early in the game

Visit the Vault Finance Career Channel at **www.vault.com/finance** – with
insider firm profiles, message boards, the Vault Finance Job Board and more.

VAULT CAREER
LIBRARY   **47**

is key to calling attention to yourself and your desire to work in private wealth management.

It's important to note that since many firms hire full-time employees from their summer internship programs, there are less opportunities available in the fall of one's senior year of college or last year of graduate business school. Thus, ideally, candidates for full-time positions should consider a private banking summer internship during the summer after their junior year in college, or the summer after their first year in business school, in the hopes of getting a full-time offer that starts after they graduate.

Typically, the full-time and summer intern recruiting cycle for the largest firms in the industry is as follows:

- November to December after junior year of college or first year of graduate business school: Candidates for summer internships attend information sessions and other recruiting events to get information about the division(s) they're interested in.

- December to March: Interview for a summer position.

- June to August: Summer internship.

- August to September: Those who didn't receive an offer from the firm where they interned, or those who want to explore options at other firms, attend recruiting events and start applying for other full-time positions.

- October to December: Interview for a full-time job that starts after graduation.

Unlike the more institutionalized sales and trading desks at most banks and investment companies, private banking is somewhat easier to break into using contacts that may already be working in the industry, especially in smaller firms. Private bankers often pride themselves on being good judges of people, and if you already know someone within a firm (and they like you), they may readily put in a good word for you.

Private wealth management branches within a larger Wall Street firm or money-center bank can sometimes recruit from other parts of the company, especially for the more specialized positions. For example, an equity strategist within the research department or asset management arm of a major firm could move to the private bank.

Traders can sometimes seek to move into private wealth management. It's generally perceived to be less stressful than working the trading desk, and can still have an entrepreneurial streak. The PWM firms, however, will be very careful to ensure that the trader has the judgment and interpersonal skills necessary to hand-hold their high-net-worth clients.

At most firms, the human resources department brings in the entry-level people, both graduate and undergraduate. Most firms will have vice presidents signing off on associate-level hires, especially if they'll be working closely together in a regional office.

Visit the Vault Finance Career Channel at **www.vault.com/finance** – with
insider firm profiles, message boards, the Vault Finance Job Board and more.

VAULT CAREER LIBRARY   **49**

Resumes and Cover Letters

CHAPTER 6

The Resume

Your resume is your first impression to people who have never shook your hand or looked you in the eye, and it should reflect complete professionalism. Wall Street firms in general review thousands of resumes every year, so yours should stand out—but not because of an eye-catching font or different colored paper.

At private wealth management firms, most collegians have a finance or business background, which is expected. For undergraduates, that will mean business or economics courses, even if they aren't your major, along with internships or summer work that reflects a desire to enter finance. That can be teller work at a small local bank, internships at an investment firm, or any kind of management experience, especially if it combines people skills with financial responsibilities. One private banker recalls that his recruiter was excited about how he went back to his summer job each year in his small town and ultimately became a mid-level summer manager—at Burger King. But think about it: It's a job that combines sales, personnel management, financial responsibilities and customer service. The leap from French fries to options hedging strategies can be shorter than you think.

Whatever is on your resume, make sure that you've kept busy. While compassionate and caring, private bankers are also very ambitious and driven. A resume that shows a token internship and membership in a fraternity or sorority won't be enough. Campus leaders are preferred, whether they've run the school paper, were elected class president, or headed up the campus chapter of Amnesty International. And be sure you did something noteworthy in those roles, too.

Perhaps unlike other Wall Street positions, private wealth management firms also like to see public service or philanthropy on your resume. High-net-worth individuals often find themselves giving to charities, even if only for the tax benefits, and someone with personal experience working on behalf of a charity can add perspective to the client's decision making. More and more

Visit the Vault Finance Career Channel at **www.vault.com/finance** – with insider firm profiles, message boards, the Vault Finance Job Board and more.

VAULT CAREER LIBRARY   51

firms are bringing in specialists to help their clients give away money (thank you, Bill Gates and Warren Buffett), but the banker can help start the conversation through his own work.

The same advice applies to those in business school, but there's an added opportunity to emphasize your post-undergrad work, whatever it may be. Ideally, you have some financial industry experience that can be brought to bear, even if it's in accounting. Emphasize not just your skills, but also your drive and initiative through ideas and projects you've worked on.

On-campus recruiting being what it is, you may not necessarily have to present a cover letter, but it's a good idea to craft one regardless, especially if the firm you'd prefer doesn't make it out to your college. Think hard about why you want a job in private wealth management. If it's just about the money, HR will likely forward you along to sales and trading. Profit isn't evil, of course—this is still Wall Street. And while a successful career in private wealth management can put you on par with at least some of your clients by the time you retire, this isn't the movie *Wall Street*. Emphasize a desire to work closely with people to make the most out of their wealth. Teamwork and an entrepreneurial drive will certainly catch someone's eye as well.

Sample Private Wealth Management Resume

Johnny G. Doe

---

23 Wintergarden Lane • Edgewater, NJ 07020
201-555-1212 • jdoe@gmail.com

OBJECTIVE

To gain an analyst-level position, with the opportunity for advancement and growth, at a private wealth management firm.

EDUCATION

Yale University, New Haven, CT
Bachelor of Arts in economics, with a minor in sociology, expected May 2007
Current GPA: 3.2
Major GPA: 3.7

EXPERIENCE

Intern, HSBC Private Bank, New York, May to August 2006

• Learned the inner workings of a private wealth management firm during a 12-week internship.

• Assisted analysts and associates in creating research and meeting materials for clients.

• Researched areas including real estate investment trusts, real estate tax law, fixed-income instruments and equities.

President, Yale University Investment Club, September 2006 to present

• Lead a 50-student club aimed at managing a portion of the University's endowment.

• Discovered a fixed-income product that gave the endowment a 25 basis point improvement in performance.

Visit the Vault Finance Career Channel at **www.vault.com/finance** – with
insider firm profiles, message boards, the Vault Finance Job Board and more.

V/\ULT CAREER LIBRARY   53

• Managed all club meetings and activities, along with the club's relationship with the Chancellor's office.

Assistant Manager, Macy's, Garden State Plaza, Paramus, NJ, Summer 2004 and 2005

• Served as the No. 2 manager in the men's department of one of the biggest Macy's stores in the Northeast.

• Managed employees, schedules and day to day operations of the department and assisted with budgeting and purchasing.

• Handled customer inquiries and complaints.

Mentor, Big Brothers Big Sisters program, Fort Lee, NJ, 2001 to present

• Served as a big brother to three teens from broken homes, helping with homework and providing a positive role model.

• Marketed the program to the greater Edgewater and Fort Lee areas.

• Aided in creating the program budget over the last two fiscal years.

SKILLS

Proficient in all Microsoft Office products and most major financial database software. Fluent in Spanish, and can speak French acceptably.

Sample Private Wealth Management Cover Letter

23 Wintergarden Ln.
Edgewater, NJ 07020

Sept. 29, 2006

Ms. Maria Enriques
Vice President of MBA & MA Recruiting
ABC Private Bank
ABC Holdings Inc.
99 51st St.
New York, NY 10001

Ms. Enriques:

On the recommendation of ABC Private Bank's recruiter, Thomas Paine, I am writing to apply for a position as an analyst at ABC Private Bank. I believe my solid financial experience and my outgoing, compassionate personality would make me a strong addition to the ABC Private Bank team.

I am due to graduate this spring from Yale University with a B.A. in economics and a major GPA of 3.7. I also have a minor in sociology. The combination of these disciplines gives me a stronger view of finance and the marketplace than they would separately.

I interned last year at HSBC Private Bank in New York, and am thus very familiar with the workings of a major private wealth management firm. While HSBC has expressed an interest in having me back upon graduation, I believe that ABC Private Bank, with its team-based approach to managing clients' holdings and its more ethical compensation structure, would be a better place to work. Nonetheless, exposure to HSBC's private wealth management arm gave me valuable experience in the field and a greater appreciation of the work private bankers do for their high-net-worth clients.

In addition to my academic and internship work, I have been a member of the Yale University Investment Club during my entire academic

Visit the Vault Finance Career Channel at **www.vault.com/finance** – with
insider firm profiles, message boards, the Vault Finance Job Board and more.

V∧ULT CAREER LIBRARY   **55**

career, and have just been elected president of the club. We currently manage 10 percent of the University's endowment, and our returns last year surpassed that of the endowment's other managers by 37 basis points. Last spring, I also brought a new fixed-income investment vehicle to the attention of the endowment's managers that brought about a 25 basis point improvement in the endowment's overall returns.

In my spare time, I serve as a mentor through my local Big Brothers Big Sisters program, and I'm active in charitable activities through my church as well. I have worked my way through college on scholarships and summer jobs, and rose to the rank of assistant manager at Macy's during the two summers before my internship.

I am a hard worker who has earned what I've received, and my academic knowledge and real-life experience can make me a valuable part of ABC Private Bank.

Thank you for your time and consideration. I look forward to your reply.

Sincerely,
John Doe

Unlike cover letters for some other jobs, don't say you're going to call the employer to follow up. Ask your recruiter about it, but frankly, if you're good enough, they'll call you, never fear. They have enough going on without you ringing the phone constantly. The recruiter will serve as a fine contact for that sort of thing.

The Interview

CHAPTER 7

The Interview Process

The interview process for full-time and summer internship positions in wealth management starts either on campus, when you sign up to meet with the recruiter, or after you've sent in your resume and are contacted for your first interview. Generally, the first interview is somewhat informal, especially at the college level, though you should always act professionally.

Most large firms target 10 to 12 campuses for full-time entry-level recruitment efforts, usually in September or October of the final school year. After first-round interviews, the human resources department sifts through all the resumes and interview notes to find those candidates they want to bring into the office.

Second interviews also happen in the fall, and candidates are often flown to New York, or wherever the main office is, for the occasion. If there's a third interview required, they will typically occur during October or November. Soon after second- or third-round interviews, you'll have a yes or no.

The interview process for summer internships usually occurs later than that for full-time positions.

Interview questions

The interview is a very detailed dance at most private wealth management firms, with the questions well thought out and structured, and the answers scrutinized carefully. Especially for entry-level positions, a good interview can be the top deciding factor in hiring. "I don't care necessarily what their degree is in. I want to know what makes them tick," says one frequent HR interviewer at a private wealth management firm.

As with most Wall Street interviews, you can expect a series of very general questions as well as some questions to determine your financial acumen. However, you'll find that the interview can be more personal at times, with your interviewer asking about hobbies and social matters. You'll also be given some situational questions unique to private wealth management.

Visit the Vault Finance Career Channel at **www.vault.com/finance** – with insider firm profiles, message boards, the Vault Finance Job Board and more.

VAULT CAREER LIBRARY   57

You won't find some of the bluster or bravado that you might have experienced interviewing for trading desk jobs or investment banking. Private bankers are still masters of the universe, but that universe is the client, and the client is treated with deep respect. The customer-focused aspects of the business will come through in a very professional, genial interview, for the most part, though the questions can and will be tough.

Sample Interview Questions: General Questions

Why do you want a career in private wealth management?

While private wealth management has grown in popularity as a career choice in recent years, it's still perceived as a smaller cousin to the other Wall Street opportunities. Investment bankers chart the fate of major corporations, while traders can have millions of dollars riding on their actions. Private wealth management? Why would you want to hold Aunt Matilda's hand while working with her on a boring fixed income portfolio for her and her cat? Or for that matter, is the allure of catering to an ultra-rich movie star or famous CEO your primary motivation? (If so, best to back away slowly right now. Those jobs are the most important in any PWM firm, and you just won't get those clients for many years.) Show that you understand what private wealth management is, what attracts you to the job, and the opportunities you see there for your own career growth, as well as the growth of the industry itself.

So what led you to this company?

You should familiarize yourself not only with the firm you're interviewing with, but also a number of other private banks as well, for comparison's sake. At a private bank that's part of a Wall Street firm or financial giant, certainly the reputation of the company is a factor, since you know you'll get exposure to the best in the business. For smaller firms, it's time to talk about the entrepreneurial spirit and the personal touch. Check out the latest private wealth management rankings in magazines like the *Robb Report*, *Worth*, or *Euromoney*. Go through the firm's web site for more details. Know what you're talking about.

What are your greatest strengths?

This is a good place to emphasize not only your financial know-how, but also your personal side. Private wealth management firms want to see someone who's patient, compassionate and cognizant of the responsibility they have in managing someone's fortune. They want someone able to take complex issues and break them down so that average people understand them. Don't get too touchy-feely, but definitely emphasize interpersonal skills.

What are your greatest weaknesses?

Never answer this question with anything remotely unflattering. Impatience is going to be a problem for your candidacy. A lack of social graces will doom you. If you failed math, that's probably not ideal either. Saying that you don't have weaknesses could sound a little too cocky—fine for the guys in the boiler room, but private bankers need a bit more circumspection than that. A difficulty with English lit classes or a propensity toward too much coffee would do nicely, but don't try to be overly witty, and be careful that your answer can't backfire on you.

What skills do you have that make you a good candidate for our program?

Time to get specific with class work, job experience and those interpersonal skills. Be sure to highlight those items mentioned on your resume, and go into those experiences in greater detail. Good problem-solving and analytical skills are important, as is an ability to network and come up with new projects or ideas. You want to present yourself as someone with some good, raw skills in economics and finance, but also as someone who can work a room, listen quietly when need be and act compassionately.

What motivates you?

Yes, greed is good. You can certainly say that the entrepreneurial aspects of the job appeal to you. The money is good, but that's a given for any job on Wall Street. The concept of really helping people to better their lives is a good one, as long as you can pull it off without sounding corny. Something to the effect of, "I do feel like I'm a self-starter, very entrepreneurial, and the opportunity to build a client base, a business really, is very attractive. And yes, money helps. But with this firm, I find the notion of working with people

Visit the Vault Finance Career Channel at **www.vault.com/finance** – with
insider firm profiles, message boards, the Vault Finance Job Board and more.

VAULT CAREER LIBRARY   **59**

who have worked so hard for their money, helping them manage it and have a better life, that's really compelling."

What are some of your outside interests?

Not that you'll have time to pursue them once you get a job, but feel free to discuss whatever you do to blow off steam, challenge your mind, improve your health or just relax. The interviewer is looking for a more balanced person, since they tend to have better interpersonal skills and can more easily relate to a client's complex needs than someone who goes to school then day-trades the rest of the time.

Are you a risk taker?

Very tricky question, this one. High-net-worth clients may have become rich by taking big risks, but now that they are rich, that desire to put it all on the line over and over understandably wanes. Most clients want to ensure they and their families have plenty of money to live on for years to come, and aren't about to chase massive returns. The best answer is to discuss risk as a part of life, and that yes, sometimes you have to take risk—even enjoy it, at times. However, you should note that there are solid, well-informed risks and stupid risks. You prefer the former.

Where do you want to be in five years?

You really want to say "right here" without really saying that. If you're an undergrad, it's perfectly OK to mention that you might want to pursue your MBA, but otherwise, you should say that you want to be in private wealth management in some capacity, working with clients and helping them with their financial issues.

Sample Interview Questions: Finance Questions

Where do you see the markets going this year?

Time to drop the touchy-feely bit and talk nuts and bolts. Show that you're keeping up with the markets, reading the *Journal* and watching something more on CNBC besides Jim Cramer. And don't just talk about stocks, mention bonds, cash investments, commodities, overseas markets—anything you can reasonably discuss without getting in over your head. Also, be sure to discuss the economic underpinnings of it all, such as consumer spending and the Federal Reserve's interest rate policy.

The Powerball's up to $25 million. What would you do with that?

This question is designed to see just how well you've done your homework on private wealth management. Be honest about your own personal experience— if you're young and single, then feel free to say you'll get a nice Central Park apartment, but also note that you'll need to plan for a (hopefully) long life with a good balance of stocks and bonds that can be adjusted over time, and throw in some philanthropy. Then go on to say how that would change once you got married and had kids, especially with college costs these days. Talk about creating trusts for the kids, planning for your estate and taking care of elderly parents. In essence, project yourself over time and cover those bases. You don't have to get too technical or discuss individual products, though mentioning the company's flagship product may be a good move. However, avoid the temptation to get too detailed and, as a result, get in over your head.

How are your parents doing on their retirement savings?

Again, be honest. If it's just a 401(k), that's fine. Talk about how you'd balance that in this market, and revisit it again next year when the market turns. You should also discuss whatever other products or investments they have, and feel free to mention what you wish they had.

Sample Interview Questions: Situational Questions

What's the most important trait for a private banker to possess?

Here's where they separate the wheat from the chaff. Protecting capital while maximizing returns based on a risk profile is OK. Being an advocate for your

Visit the Vault Finance Career Channel at **www.vault.com/finance** – with
insider firm profiles, message boards, the Vault Finance Job Board and more.

VAULT CAREER LIBRARY   61

client is a far better answer. These firms exist for, and because of, the client. The term "customer service" doesn't even begin to come close to the kind of attention, advice and advocacy clients expect. A client-centric answer will serve you far better than a financial one.

You propose what you believe is a very strong investment opportunity to your client, but he balks. What do you do?

Anybody who keeps on with a hard sell is heading in the wrong direction. Given that you think this opportunity fits within the client's overall strategy, disagreements like this should lead to a review of the client's goals. Maybe he's changed his thinking in recent weeks or months, in which case you've gleaned important information about your client's needs. Maybe the client simply doesn't see how the opportunity fits into his strategy, and a review of goals and strategy could help him see it in a more positive light. Ultimately, however, when it comes to this kind of "optional" opportunity, it's the client's call. It can be revisited in the future if you feel strongly about it, but for now, if he's not buying, let it go.

You believe very strongly that your client should hedge against risk in his portfolio through a certain vehicle, but your client is interested in something else that may run counter to his long-term goals? What do you do?

The difference between this question and the last is deceptively profound, as this is structured as a far more important issue than a simple chance to make a buck. Once again, differences should be taken as an opportunity to review those long-term goals, and the pros and cons of the competing approaches should be explored in detail. You should be unafraid to say that this is a bad idea. You may also want to put your client in direct contact with the appropriate specialists at your firm, like the market strategist, so they can get a second opinion. In this case, the decision might cost the client, but as long as it's not going to ruin him, you may have to reluctantly go along with it, then start planning the exit strategy—or the recovery strategy.

Your client wants to do something exceptionally ill-advised, like pouring all his money into a company that is, at best, a high-risk venture. What do you do?

Once again, start with the goals and review. Bring in the specialists as needed. Try to find some alternative plans of action that may satisfy whatever it is that prompted the move, yet would at least preserve more capital. Yet again, you can't stop someone from ruining themselves if they want. In this case, though, ensure that the client has discussed the move with all affected parties, including his family and anyone who may have a financial stake in the move. Express your opinion freely to all of them. If the client still goes through with it, get the exit strategy in place and, ideally, get the client to sign off on it right away, so that the losses are minimized as much as possible.

Your Turn: Questions to Ask the Interviewers

Private wealth management firms want inquisitive minds, and generally welcome smart questions during interviews, the key word being smart. You need to do your homework about the company before sitting down in the interview chair. That way you'll ask better questions and won't be embarrassed when the interviewer says, "Well, that's right up on our web site."

There are things, however, that private banks won't discuss through publicly available materials. So take a look at these questions, see if they're answered online or through your school's career office, and if they're not, ask them at the interview.

What would be my role here? Can you give me a sense of what an average day is like?

The purpose of this question is multilayered. You want to know how the company's inner workings are structured, so that you can find out if you'll be on your own as a private banker (or supporting a private banker as an analyst) with access to the firm's specialists, if you'll be in a two-person partnership or if you'll be supporting one private banker, catering to clients. A few firms go with team approaches, and you'll want to know how you fit in that team structure.

Visit the Vault Finance Career Channel at **www.vault.com/finance** – with
insider firm profiles, message boards, the Vault Finance Job Board and more.

VAULT CAREER LIBRARY   **63**

Are there opportunities for advancement? Specialization in a particular field?

You're looking ahead to your end-game with this question, so be careful how you ask it. Don't appear too eager to climb the ladder. Make it seem as though you really want to spend the rest of your life at this firm. You know it may not be true, and they know it as well, but the appearance is at least helpful. And you're actually trying to find out how much turnover they have there. If your interviewer talks a lot about patience and teamwork, then you're going to be in the same role a while—but on the other hand, with turnover low, it could also be an excellent place to work and grow. A firm that "brings people along quickly" could be doing so because nobody wants to work there—or they're growing by leaps and bounds. Follow-ups are key here. Ask why they do what they do.

The specialization question is another way of gauging what kind of future you may have there, as well as the kind of resources a firm may have at your disposal. If you'd love to focus on fixed income investments, learning that they have a team of fixed income specialists tells you that they have the resources necessary to specialize to a degree, and that you have another avenue for advancement there.

Without getting into numbers, can you tell me how compensation is structured here?

It's generally bad form to ask numbers—they'll tell you if they like you, especially if you initially beg off as the question above did. What you're trying to do here is see how much of your income would come from a base salary and how much comes from bonuses or commissions. You also want to know how you get those bonuses and commissions. If you're an investment guru, then a commission-based compensation plan may work best if you can build your clients' portfolios into cash machines. Bonuses for attracting new assets to the firm are a good way for a networker and schmoozer to earn big bucks. And if it's a performance metric based on how satisfied your clients are, then someone with strengths in interpersonal relationships will do well.

Some private bankers get uneasy with the prospect of hustling the company's proprietary financial products like a common broker, and some firms have put a stop to the practice due to the inherent conflicts of interest that can create. If you get a bonus for putting your client into your firm's mutual funds, that's fine, but your compensation shouldn't be based in large part on doing so.

Are there opportunities for ongoing education?

If you don't have your MBA, this is a great question to ask. While most private wealth management firms will move you from analyst to associate without an MBA, knowing that the firm may help pay for it can be a powerful incentive. Some firms want all their private bankers to have advanced degrees, even if it's just for the prestige of saying that, yes, all of their private bankers have advanced degrees. In the same vein, some firms will send you off to get certified by every private or public group possible, so that you'll end up as a CPA, CFA, you name it.

Others, however, have internal training in place, and prefer to see you trained in-house rather than sent off for courses or certifications that may or may not have bearing on what the firm needs. Be wary, certainly, of the small firm that says it has extensive in-house training. Frankly, it might simply not want to send promising young private bankers off to grad school for a year or two. But if a large money-center bank or investment house says it prefers in-house training, you should believe them. It'll be extensive and probably tougher than getting an MBA or CFA certification. And some firms see a more mercenary advantage to in-house training—it's less portable should you decide to leave the company.

Let the Education Begin

After you're hired, you'll receive your introduction to the firm, which will likely make you feel like you never left school. You'll spend anywhere from two to six months learning about the firm, its products and service offerings, its regulations and its philosophies. The time is generally shorter for associates, who already have either experience or an MBA, and much longer for analysts, who are learning from the ground up.

If you're an analyst, you'll also be preparing for your Series 7 and Series 63 or 66 tests, which will be a large part of your classroom work. Depending on whom you talk to, the Series 7 is horribly difficult ... or just merely hard. Firms will give you all the information you need to know to pass these tests, but you'll still need to study diligently. Some people don't pass the first time, but some firms will look askance at flunking and they'll generally give you one more chance. Flunk twice, and you're out of there.

Visit the Vault Finance Career Channel at **www.vault.com/finance** – with
insider firm profiles, message boards, the Vault Finance Job Board and more.

V/\ULT CAREER LIBRARY **65**

By the time you're done with training, you should have a solid grasp on how your firm prefers to manage accounts. You'll know which instruments and products are favored and which specialists within the firm to call upon for help. However, while you'll certainly be told a great deal about customer service and managing the clients, nothing will prepare you for the day when you finally sit down in front of a wealthy individual and talk about how they want to manage their money.

ON THE JOB

Life on the Job

CHAPTER 8

It's All About the Clients

As much as the place you work will help you define your career in private wealth management, your clients will shape your day-to-day working life. Count yourself fortunate, too, because you'll be dealing with some of the most interesting people you've ever met. Your clients may have worked hard all their lives for their money, became instant millionaires in the dot-com era (and didn't lose it), inherited their money from family or even hit it big in the lottery. No matter how they got it, they're almost uniformly fascinating people who want to put their wealth to work. And you may even learn a thing or two from them, no matter who they are.

Very few clients are what one private banker calls "the wacky rich." According to the Spectrem Group's annual survey, there were a record 8.3 million U.S. millionaires in 2005. The majority of those are simply people who saved their entire lives and have homes and retirement assets worth more than $1 million in value. Households worth $5 million or more—your potential client base—grew 26 percent in 2005 to 930,000. While these are now considered truly high-net-worth clients, the vast majority of them are simply hardworking people in generally lucrative lines of work, from medicine to law to business.

In short, these are smart, driven, successful people who worked hard for their money. They aren't going to want to do anything wacky with the fortune they toiled so hard to garner. Only a small percentage of private wealth management clients are even known to the public at large, though there are certainly top corporate executives, wealthy politicians, sports stars and entertainers among private banking clients around the world. These are few and far between, however, so if you're thinking of a jet-setting lifestyle of being a private banker to the stars, bear in mind that such a scenario is an extreme exception to the rule.

That said, large firms such as Goldman Sachs and Lehman Brothers do compete heavily for the fortunate few whose net worth can be measured in hundreds of millions, or even billions. And the importance of keeping that client happy won't be just your personal and professional priority, but a top priority of your firm.

Visit the Vault Finance Career Channel at **www.vault.com/finance** – with insider firm profiles, message boards, the Vault Finance Job Board and more.

VAULT CAREER LIBRARY   69

Relationships vary

Your relationship to your clients will be as varied as the personalities involved. In some cases, private bankers become trusted confidants in many areas beyond the financial. A good private banker can earn the respect and admiration of clients and their families, and in some cases become friends over the long run, after years of solid advice and faithful service. Private bankers can be there for the best and worst of a client's life, and some people truly appreciate that.

Other clients, however, just don't want that kind of relationship with their money managers, and that's fine, too. You're still there to help them with absolutely whatever they need, but if they don't want to tell you why they want something, then so be it. You're not there to be their friend, after all. You're there to provide them with the kind of service only top dollar can buy.

Likewise, clients have different approaches when it comes to dealing with the management of their wealth. At one extreme, some clients simply want to hand off their affairs, much like the British gentlemen of the Victorian era handed off their finances to a barrister, since such things were "beneath them." Other clients will want a say in the smallest minutiae of their management plans. Some will want a minimum of fuss; others will want to consult the entire firm's slate of experts.

One private banker's client list reads like a list of Fortune 500 executives (and thus, his name won't be used here), and has even served as a private banker to someone many, many rungs up the corporate ladder at his own company. The level of friendship and involvement varies, from "let's golf this weekend" and "call me the minute it drops below $50 per share," to "thank you, we'll talk next month." But his one constant is that all of these people are uniformly intelligent, savvy and knowledgeable when it comes to investments.

"I liken it to a chess game," he says. "There are sort of five to 10 topics that might come up, and I think through eight moves in advance on any one of those topics. Because as soon as you bring up a topic, chances are they're automatically thinking through seven moves down the path. If you don't have that eighth move ..."

Managing your clients

Indeed, planning ahead is a keystone of successful private wealth management. If your client asks a question you're unprepared to answer, his or her confidence in you is taken down a notch. However, if you can present multiple scenarios, and plans based on those scenarios, you come across as knowledgeable, helpful and genuinely interested in helping the client manage his or her wealth.

Of course, there are times when your client will disagree with what you believe is sound advice. And there are stories within private wealth management circles, probably somewhat apocryphal, of the catastrophic blunders this or that client made despite the best efforts of his private banker. Thankfully, such abject incompetence on the part of the client is rare—they had to have some smarts to make all that money, after all.

A Day in the Life: Analyst at a Wall Street Firm

Analyst with a large Wall Street firm's private wealth management arm

8:00 a.m.: I like to get in early, so if I'm not stuck on the subway, I'm already in the office. There's always something that someone laid on me the night before, so I want to check it over or, more likely, finish it up.

8:30 a.m.: Our section of the building is usually completely up and running by 8:30 a.m. I'm usually fielding e-mails from an associate or vice president on the work I've been doing for them. Recently, I've become the supposed fixed income expert, so I've been pulling up historicals on the performance of short- and long-term corporates, investment (grade) and junk (grade), whenever the Treasury yield curve has inverted, like it's done a few times already this year.

9:00 a.m.: We all listen in to the conference call on the morning's trades. I like hearing what the experts think and comparing it to what I think is going to happen. Most of the time, I agree with the experts. When I don't, it's about 50-50, me winning half the time. Nobody says it's an exact science, and even the top guys on Wall Street can be wrong.

Visit the Vault Finance Career Channel at **www.vault.com/finance** – with
insider firm profiles, message boards, the Vault Finance Job Board and more.

V/\ULT CAREER LIBRARY   **71**

9:30 a.m.: This is generally a pretty big deadline on any given day for the research we do, because the associates will want the research for their calls and meetings later in the day, once the market starts. Usually it's a rush to get things done. You can tell who's done the all-nighters and who hasn't.

10:00 a.m.: I settle in and get some more research done. One associate wants some portfolio projections, another wants some comparisons of different hedge funds, and somebody else is still hoping for that inverted yield curve study.

11:05 a.m.: One of the associates e-mails me with a question about a piece of research I did a few days ago. He's on a call with a client, but it's appeared he's glossed things over at the moment, but now I have to rush to find the answer. Thank God, it turns out he missed a footnote in what I wrote, and it's nothing I did. I e-mail him back, and he's kind enough to acknowledge that he missed it. Not all of them are that nice.

12:30 p.m.: Lunch. The analysts usually head out together, more or less, unless someone's crunching on something. Occasionally, an associate or VP who liked something we did will take us out. That's always nice, because it's a pretty good meal, but it also means that they'll probably hit you with something even more difficult to do down the road. Or before dessert.

1:30 p.m.: Back from lunch. More research.

2:00 p.m.: Class time. The firm wants us to learn as much as possible about a variety of investments, which makes sense to me, since we're going to be advising clients eventually on everything from hedge funds to real estate to Asian equities. Today it's the latest thinking in estate planning, and how to best use the new tax laws to preserve as much as possible. The resident associate expert starts in, and then one of the analysts gives a PowerPoint talk, after which he's grilled by everyone from the analysts to the VPs, and even an MD or two. We're usually doing one of these once every quarter or so, and it's a month of hell beforehand. You have to know your topic cold and be ready for anything.

3:30 p.m.: An associate who I did some last-minute work for agreed to let me sit in on the client meeting—my little reward. I'm the dutiful assistant, getting coffee for everyone, taking notes. The associate lets me explain the work I did—I didn't expect that—and the client says "nice job" when I'm done. The client is old-school Wall Street, so I'm pretty sure he knows what that can mean to an analyst. Even when I try to be cynical, it's still nice to hear.

4:30 p.m.: The closing bell. I stop what I'm doing to see how the day went and if it's going to affect anything that I'm working on. Some of the newer analysts have to drop everything to do some technical analysis work on the day's trading in just about everything—stocks, bonds, commodities, you name it. The rest of us use it as a good excuse to grab coffee, usually with a shopping list in hand for the associates and VPs. Then, it's back to work.

6:30 p.m.: Decision time. If I'm ahead of the game and there's nothing pressing, I usually try to take off around this time. If I'm crunching on something, I'll order dinner and keep plugging away. I really like to get out most nights, even if it means I procrastinate—which usually means that when I do stay, I'm there until midnight or later.

A Day in the Life: PWM Associate at a Major Banking Corporation

6:00 a.m.: Wake up. My day starts like a lot of other people's on Wall Street. I get up, check my BlackBerry for messages, and log in at home with my coffee to check up on anything that may have happened overnight with a client or an investment. On my way in, it's either the *Journal* or some catch-up work on the laptop.

7:00 a.m.: Arrive at office. I'm usually in by 7 a.m. or so. From then until about 8 a.m., I'm reviewing the overnight developments abroad. I have a few clients in some global investments and some real estate overseas. If a client is overseas and I need to check in with them, I'll do that then.

8:00-9:00 a.m.: The day's data and earnings come in and are reviewed.

9:00 a.m.: The morning call. Our investment strategists come in over the old squawk box—well, it's a conference call now—around 9. We get the latest thinking from the entire firm, not just the private bank, which has very good strategists, but also the larger research arm, too. Most days, there's nothing huge that I have to react strongly to. Most of the time, if there's up or down action expected in a major holding on the part of one of my clients, I'll already have seen that coming and will have a strategy in place. If it's unexpected and a big enough development, I'll get on the phone before the

Visit the Vault Finance Career Channel at **www.vault.com/finance** – with insider firm profiles, message boards, the Vault Finance Job Board and more.

VAULT CAREER LIBRARY   **73**

open with a few options for them, and we'll decide if there's anything we want to do. Likewise, if there's a pending development that fits in with a client's strategy, and I think we should jump on it, I'll call then too. Again, that's pretty rare, but it does happen.

9:30 a.m.: The opening bell. By the time trading opens in New York, I've made sure that my clients' positions are still valid across the board. I have multiple strategies in place for each and every investment my clients have, so if I've had to execute on one of them, I'll go ahead and place the order for it when I think it's best to move during the day. Otherwise, once we get the opening bell, I'm pretty much settled in and can think about the bigger stuff.

10:00 a.m.: Meeting with members of the firm's capital team. I got one client right now, for example, that owns outright a house in the Hamptons and is trying to lay on a $1 million mortgage. The house is worth $8 million. So I have to make sure that's proceeding along with our capital people.

11:30 a.m.: Client calls, with varying degrees of success. Some are there and happy, some are playing phone tag. One client, a real estate family, just had a major liquidity event. We're trying to set up a meeting to talk about that event and what they want to do with it.

1:00 p.m.: Lunch, with a client, to discuss hedging strategies and the current market, trying to get the firm's chief investment officer or an investment strategist to join at the last minute.

2:30 p.m.: New business and more client calls. I just sent out a response to a proposal from a major New York-area charity, a referral from one of my happy clients. He's on the charity's board, and he teed things up for me with the charity president, the head of the finance committee and the head of the investment committee.

The rest of the day is spent on a variety of things, whether it's client meetings or calls, working with ongoing projects, planning ahead or drumming up new business. I check the markets regularly throughout the day, and our firm has regular updates via e-mail as well. If there's an unexpected occurrence, I'm back to the portfolios and reviewing options to see if there's a need to make a move.

4:00 p.m.: The closing bell. The next 30 to 45 minutes is spent doing a thorough check of the day's activity, as well as afternoon earnings reports. I check in at the close, and pay attention to any earnings from companies that my clients have an interest in. Then it's back to everything else.

4:45 p.m.: More client calls. I check in with my clients as much as we both feel comfortable with. Some people are very much into having me call all I want, others will only want me to call to set up something at a predetermined time, or when there's a crisis that I haven't been empowered to deal with on my own.

7:00 p.m.: Leave the office. I don't have too many West Coast clients, so I'm usually out of the office between 6 and 7 in the evening. I try to take some work home with me on the train, except for Friday nights. It's really rare that I'll get a late call or a weekend call. Some of my colleagues do, but my clients are generally pretty sophisticated, and they don't need me 24/7. And they sure aren't doing anything rash with their money on a Saturday.

I do some evenings now and then, though, whether it's a client meeting or a networking thing. I am involved in charity, which is not only good for the soul, but provides outstanding opportunities for business. When I do endowment work, too, it usually means all the black-tie events and the golf outings, but those are happening with people who are potential clients.

More Comments from the PWM Associate

"I try to set up multiple scenarios for my clients with each of their major investments. I try to think 10 steps ahead for them, so that when there's an event in the market, or in their lives, I'm right there with ready-to-go options. And those options and scenarios have to be constantly reviewed and updated for each client's investment. For something like stock market moves, I try to get those preapproved when I sit down with my client, so that I'm not on the phone trying to find them when the market is tanking. Same with bonds or any easily tradable investment.

But I'm also thinking about their real estate, their tangible assets, and planning ahead for them, whether it's estate planning, possible loan needs, getting kids through college, marriage, divorce, whatever. Yeah, someone will always come up with something completely new for me to consider, but the more things I'm ready for, the better I can

Visit the Vault Finance Career Channel at **www.vault.com/finance** – with insider firm profiles, message boards, the Vault Finance Job Board and more.

VAULT CAREER LIBRARY   **75**

serve my client's needs, and the happier that client is. That brings in the referrals, like the endowment work.

I do meet regularly with the other people in the firm. Like with the mortgage of the house in the Hamptons, I'm working with our capital team to make sure the client's getting the best deal possible. I had a client that was going to make a major philanthropic effort, and I worked weeks with our experts on that. Our investment strategists are constantly reviewing client portfolios right along with me, and I may sit down with them to go over some things. If I've got some ideas for estate planning, I'll bounce it off the lawyers. Come October-November, we're already working with the tax team, and we'll do that through March if need be. We have a good team here.

Of course, my boss is in touch quite a bit, too. We have formal sit-down reviews of all the clients' activities on a regular basis, but she's up to speed on my clients and their investments, and we talk about potential moves."

A Day in the Life of a Small-Firm Private Banker

Vice President in charge of a regional office

4:00 a.m.: Get up. My day begins early, when I get up and review everything that came in the night before. Since we don't have a massive equity strategy team, I'm constantly reviewing outside research on my clients' holdings, which we subscribe to. I spend most of my morning reading up to see what the latest thinking is. I stay glued to the TV and PC at home because I'm on the West Coast and I don't want to be commuting when the market opens.

6:30 a.m.: The opening bell.

7:30 a.m.: Once the market is open and I'm OK with what's going on, then I shower and get dressed and everything else, and head into work. I got a Sirius satellite radio in the car just so I could listen to Bloomberg radio on my drive in.

8:15 a.m.: At the office, client calls. Once I get in the office, it's all about the clients. I'm on the phone, sending e-mails, planning ahead, doing everything I can to not only meet their needs, but anticipate them.

1:00 p.m.: The closing bell. The market closes at 1 p.m. my time, which is great. That allows me to get out of the office and go see clients without worrying about anybody's portfolio.

1:30 p.m.: Lunch with members of the local chamber of commerce. I belong to all the local business groups, and I'm there whenever they have conferences or luncheons or whatever. Any time I can be in a room with successful business people, I'm there. Sometimes it's afternoon, sometimes it's evening, but whenever.

2:30 p.m.: Client meeting at his office. Clients appreciate it when you go to them, and I'm there with my laptop and a wireless card so that if there are questions, I'm right there in my network pulling up their data without a problem, and they're still comfortable in their office or home.

4:00 p.m.: Back to the office for more calls, e-mails, laying in moves or strategies as needed for the following day.

5:00 p.m.: Heading home, which is unusual. If there isn't anything in the evening going on, I can be out of the office by 4 or 5 p.m., but that's usually just one or two days a week, usually Friday. My clients tend to be businesspeople, so we often meet after business hours so they can focus fully on their jobs. And I'll stay late a lot to ride herd on a major purchase or investment that I'm working on for a client.

Visit the Vault Finance Career Channel at **www.vault.com/finance** – with insider firm profiles, message boards, the Vault Finance Job Board and more.

VAULT CAREER LIBRARY   77

More Comments from the Small-Firm Private Banker

I started as an analyst and associate at one of the big private banks in New York, and I have to say, I like this a lot more. I feel much more entrepreneurial here, and I feel I can move faster when my client's money's at stake.

We're not a Citigroup or Goldman Sachs, so we don't have all of the in-house experts waiting there to help me with my clients' needs. But I have good relationships with lawyers and estate planners, with lenders, with all of the people my clients might need. I steer them in the right direction. And in return, those lenders and lawyers are steering business my way, too, when they have a high-end client come in looking for help.

When I'm talking with a client, I'll ask about their personal life whenever it's appropriate, because that can tip me off to future needs. I try to have as much real contact with clients as possible, because the more I get from them, the better off I am trying to help them. Sure, there are some clients who practically just want a statement in the mail every quarter. For those, when we have our regular meetings, I'm there with a million options for them to consider, and I'm there asking for permission to move if X, Y or Z happens.

During tax season, I'm right there with their accountant or family office, going through everything to make sure they get every penny. Even before tax season, I'm there trying to get them to make adjustments so they can save on their tax bill. Summers are generally slower, followed by spring. Fall and winter tend to be the busiest, between closing out one year and starting up another. I do most of my new business hunting in the spring and summer, with taxes in the fall and early winter, and then new portfolios and investments the rest of the winter.

Drumming Up Business

As an associate starting out at a private wealth ma may be given a handful of clients to manage, but t types of clients that will earn you major commiss castoffs from private bankers who left the firm responsibilities or just don't have time for t accounts. Expect to see relatively modest accoun into safe, income-generating fixed income portfolio accounts that will go nowhere fast.

It will be up to you, then, to get new clients, and y never have before. Everyone who's ever entered y potential client—your doctor, your family attorn friends, old mentors, even the bold-face name magazine could be worth a call. You'll attend d events and even make yourself home at a few pu district now and then. Have extra copies of your bus you'll need them.

Even after you've established yourself, you'll consta new accounts. You'll regularly ask (but not peste leads among their friends and colleagues. As you y money, you'll seek to attend more charity events yourself in philanthropy in order to meet the kind of make good clients.

As your accounts grow, there will be less cold-ca replaced by more word-of-mouth, client recommend networking. But you can never be content to simply clients. Your firm will continue to expect more fro continued rise in both responsibility and income de more and more clients to the firm.

© 2007 Vault, Inc.

Visit the Vault Finance Career Channel at www.vault.com/finance – with insider firm profiles, message boards, the Vault Finance Job Board and more.

V∧ **80**

Private Wealth Management Career Paths

The Basic Career Path

Starting as an analyst

As we've already explained, undergraduates will start at a private wealth management firm at the analyst level. Here, you can expect a lot of grunt work—research, basic mathematical or financial modeling, calling clients (or most likely their assistants) to confirm appointments with the associates, creating PowerPoint presentations and preparing routine statements.

However, don't knock the experience you'll receive as you work your way through the analyst ranks. You'll be asked to research a wide variety of financial products, which will give you a deep knowledge of what's out there when it's time to make decisions on behalf of your clients. Your superiors may ask you for judgment calls based on your research, giving you a chance to show your analytical skills. Working with clients, no matter how indirectly, lets you see how your firm tailors its approach from client to client.

As you gain seniority as an analyst, you'll sometimes be asked to help out in client meetings, whether it's simply clicking the next slide or presenting your own research to a client on behalf of an associate. You may be asked to think critically about whether new financial instruments in the marketplace—and there are dozens out every week lately—have a place in your associate's stable of chosen investments.

The hours are usually long—8 a.m. to 8 p.m. can be typical—but by the time your three years is up, you'll have the background necessary to start managing clients on your own.

Analysts strive to become associates, the cornerstones of private wealth management. As an associate, you'll be a lot like the private bankers described earlier in this chapter—you'll be managing client assets and building your own client base. Not every analyst becomes an associate, however, and there's competition from MBA graduates seeking those same jobs. If you're an analyst and did not receive an offer to become an associate at your firm—not a completely uncommon experience given the number of analysts hired each year, especially compared to the number of associate slots—then you can continue as an analyst and try again the following year. After another year or two, however, it's time to look elsewhere if you haven't moved up.

Chances are, you'll have to look at a smaller firm, because if you couldn't get in with, say, Deutsche Bank, then the folks at Morgan Stanley may not be interested. However, there are a number of smaller firms that welcome analysts with bulge bracket firm experience. Likewise, your skills may help you catch on with an asset management firm or even a hedge fund. Other analysts who find themselves without an associate spot might head back to school for their MBA.

Most firms will clue you in, subtly or otherwise, as you approach your second or third year anniversary as an analyst. If you're considered associate material, they'll urge you to apply for associate positions. If not, you may find yourself talking with your bosses about the merits of an MBA, or a position elsewhere in the company.

Moving up to associate

Once you gain the associate role, there's no real time frame for the rest of your moves up the corporate ladder, and each firm measures success in different ways. Some companies prefer to see their private bankers grow client assets as much as possible—especially using products and instruments developed by the company itself. Others will look at client satisfaction and how closely the private banker hewed to the client's stated risk profile and investment goals. Still, others will place more emphasis on growing a banker's client list through new business.

Your aptitudes in these areas will determine where you go next. In most firms, if you're an investment wizard bringing in major returns with less-than-expected risk, you'll be given more important accounts, and could in time become part of the market strategy team. If you're client-centric, you may end up in a supervisory role, helping other private bankers read their clients and build their approach. And if you're a whiz at attracting new clients, you may be tapped to open up a new branch office in another city (and you'll be appropriately compensated for the loss of any clients you may suffer as a result, at least until you have enough new clients). If you get any of these

8:15 a.m.: At the office, client calls. Once I get in the office, it's all about the clients. I'm on the phone, sending e-mails, planning ahead, doing everything I can to not only meet their needs, but anticipate them.

1:00 p.m.: The closing bell. The market closes at 1 p.m. my time, which is great. That allows me to get out of the office and go see clients without worrying about anybody's portfolio.

1:30 p.m.: Lunch with members of the local chamber of commerce. I belong to all the local business groups, and I'm there whenever they have conferences or luncheons or whatever. Any time I can be in a room with successful business people, I'm there. Sometimes it's afternoon, sometimes it's evening, but whenever.

2:30 p.m.: Client meeting at his office. Clients appreciate it when you go to them, and I'm there with my laptop and a wireless card so that if there are questions, I'm right there in my network pulling up their data without a problem, and they're still comfortable in their office or home.

4:00 p.m.: Back to the office for more calls, e-mails, laying in moves or strategies as needed for the following day.

5:00 p.m.: Heading home, which is unusual. If there isn't anything in the evening going on, I can be out of the office by 4 or 5 p.m., but that's usually just one or two days a week, usually Friday. My clients tend to be businesspeople, so we often meet after business hours so they can focus fully on their jobs. And I'll stay late a lot to ride herd on a major purchase or investment that I'm working on for a client.

More Comments from the Small-Firm Private Banker

I started as an analyst and associate at one of the big private banks in New York, and I have to say, I like this a lot more. I feel much more entrepreneurial here, and I feel I can move faster when my client's money's at stake.

We're not a Citigroup or Goldman Sachs, so we don't have all of the in-house experts waiting there to help me with my clients' needs. But I have good relationships with lawyers and estate planners, with lenders, with all of the people my clients might need. I steer them in the right direction. And in return, those lenders and lawyers are steering business my way, too, when they have a high-end client come in looking for help.

When I'm talking with a client, I'll ask about their personal life whenever it's appropriate, because that can tip me off to future needs. I try to have as much real contact with clients as possible, because the more I get from them, the better off I am trying to help them. Sure, there are some clients who practically just want a statement in the mail every quarter. For those, when we have our regular meetings, I'm there with a million options for them to consider, and I'm there asking for permission to move if X, Y or Z happens.

During tax season, I'm right there with their accountant or family office, going through everything to make sure they get every penny. Even before tax season, I'm there trying to get them to make adjustments so they can save on their tax bill. Summers are generally slower, followed by spring. Fall and winter tend to be the busiest, between closing out one year and starting up another. I do most of my new business hunting in the spring and summer, with taxes in the fall and early winter, and then new portfolios and investments the rest of the winter.

Drumming Up Business

As an associate starting out at a private wealth management firm, you may be given a handful of clients to manage, but these will not be the types of clients that will earn you major commissions. These are the castoffs from private bankers who left the firm, assumed greater responsibilities or just don't have time for these low-turnover accounts. Expect to see relatively modest accounts with money put into safe, income-generating fixed income portfolios—in other words, accounts that will go nowhere fast.

It will be up to you, then, to get new clients, and you'll hustle like you never have before. Everyone who's ever entered your life becomes a potential client—your doctor, your family attorney, your parents' friends, old mentors, even the bold-face names in your alumni magazine could be worth a call. You'll attend dinners, networking events and even make yourself home at a few pubs in the financial district now and then. Have extra copies of your business card ready— you'll need them.

Even after you've established yourself, you'll constantly be looking for new accounts. You'll regularly ask (but not pester) your clients for leads among their friends and colleagues. As you yourself earn more money, you'll seek to attend more charity events and even involve yourself in philanthropy in order to meet the kind of people who would make good clients.

As your accounts grow, there will be less cold-calling and shilling, replaced by more word-of-mouth, client recommendations and social networking. But you can never be content to simply sit on a fat list of clients. Your firm will continue to expect more from you, and your continued rise in both responsibility and income depend on bringing more and more clients to the firm.

Visit the Vault Finance Career Channel at **www.vault.com/finance** – with
insider firm profiles, message boards, the Vault Finance Job Board and more.

VAULT CAREER LIBRARY   **79**

Private Wealth Management Career Paths

The Basic Career Path

Starting as an analyst

As we've already explained, undergraduates will start at a private wealth management firm at the analyst level. Here, you can expect a lot of grunt work—research, basic mathematical or financial modeling, calling clients (or most likely their assistants) to confirm appointments with the associates, creating PowerPoint presentations and preparing routine statements.

However, don't knock the experience you'll receive as you work your way through the analyst ranks. You'll be asked to research a wide variety of financial products, which will give you a deep knowledge of what's out there when it's time to make decisions on behalf of your clients. Your superiors may ask you for judgment calls based on your research, giving you a chance to show your analytical skills. Working with clients, no matter how indirectly, lets you see how your firm tailors its approach from client to client.

As you gain seniority as an analyst, you'll sometimes be asked to help out in client meetings, whether it's simply clicking the next slide or presenting your own research to a client on behalf of an associate. You may be asked to think critically about whether new financial instruments in the marketplace—and there are dozens out every week lately—have a place in your associate's stable of chosen investments.

The hours are usually long—8 a.m. to 8 p.m. can be typical—but by the time your three years is up, you'll have the background necessary to start managing clients on your own.

Analysts strive to become associates, the cornerstones of private wealth management. As an associate, you'll be a lot like the private bankers described earlier in this chapter—you'll be managing client assets and building your own client base. Not every analyst becomes an associate, however, and there's competition from MBA graduates seeking those same jobs. If you're an analyst and did not receive an offer to become an associate at your firm—not a completely uncommon experience given the number of analysts hired each year, especially compared to the number of associate slots—then you can continue as an analyst and try again the following year. After another year or two, however, it's time to look elsewhere if you haven't moved up.

Chances are, you'll have to look at a smaller firm, because if you couldn't get in with, say, Deutsche Bank, then the folks at Morgan Stanley may not be interested. However, there are a number of smaller firms that welcome analysts with bulge bracket firm experience. Likewise, your skills may help you catch on with an asset management firm or even a hedge fund. Other analysts who find themselves without an associate spot might head back to school for their MBA.

Most firms will clue you in, subtly or otherwise, as you approach your second or third year anniversary as an analyst. If you're considered associate material, they'll urge you to apply for associate positions. If not, you may find yourself talking with your bosses about the merits of an MBA, or a position elsewhere in the company.

Moving up to associate

Once you gain the associate role, there's no real time frame for the rest of your moves up the corporate ladder, and each firm measures success in different ways. Some companies prefer to see their private bankers grow client assets as much as possible—especially using products and instruments developed by the company itself. Others will look at client satisfaction and how closely the private banker hewed to the client's stated risk profile and investment goals. Still, others will place more emphasis on growing a banker's client list through new business.

Your aptitudes in these areas will determine where you go next. In most firms, if you're an investment wizard bringing in major returns with less-than-expected risk, you'll be given more important accounts, and could in time become part of the market strategy team. If you're client-centric, you may end up in a supervisory role, helping other private bankers read their clients and build their approach. And if you're a whiz at attracting new clients, you may be tapped to open up a new branch office in another city (and you'll be appropriately compensated for the loss of any clients you may suffer as a result, at least until you have enough new clients). If you get any of these positions, you're also likely to be promoted to vice president. There's no fixed number of vice presidents at a given firm—it's purely a reflection of performance and experience.

You may find yourself, however, waiting a while for better positions to open up, or you may find it difficult to schmooze for new business. Depending on your strengths, you could end up in a variety of Wall Street jobs. For example, you could become a more traditional broker/dealer, go to work for an asset management firm or hedge fund, or even strike out on your own as an independent advisor. And if you haven't been back for your MBA, there's always that.

At any level, if you enjoy private wealth management and simply feel your current company is not the place for you, you can certainly try to move to a competing firm. Some contracts may specify which firms you can or can't go to, and there will most definitely be rules about soliciting your clients to follow you to your new home. However, if you've built a loyal client base, your replacement may have trouble keeping them, and you could find them knocking at your door regardless. And as much as competing firms like to make a show of honor amongst competitors, most private wealth management firms are quite keen to get their hands on another firm's private banker and possibly a few of that firm's clients.

If you do move to another firm, read your employment contract very carefully, and follow it to the letter. As much as you'd love to take your clients with you, for example, you could be on the hook for thousands, even millions of dollars if you solicit them to follow you, depending on the contract. It's a fine line—if a client asks, you can be free to tell them you're leaving the company for a competitor. And nothing is stopping you from attending the same charity events, golf outings and parties that you did before. Just be careful whom you give your card to.

Vice president and beyond

If you've made vice president, then you're in great shape at your firm, so long as you continue performing well and satisfying clients. Vice presidents are often tapped to assist in firmwide decision making, and you'll be in more supervisory roles, whether overseeing a team of bankers dedicated to clients focused on real estate, or taking over leadership of a branch office in Dallas or Silicon Valley. You may, at this point, be asked to specialize in a given

Visit the Vault Finance Career Channel at **www.vault.com/finance** – with insider firm profiles, message boards, the Vault Finance Job Board and more.

VAULT CAREER LIBRARY

83

investment or into portfolio management, assisting other private bankers with their work in these areas. Some firms allow you to continue managing accounts while doing this, whereas others will want you to fully focus on your supervisory duties or expertise (and will generally find other ways to remunerate you).

Finally, in the later years of your career, you may find yourself tapped to be a managing director. You'll be one of the top decision makers in your firm, helping to focus the company's overall investment strategy, client focus and/or new business strategy. Depending on your firm, you'll still have clients to oversee, but you'll generally get the most high-profile, high-net-worth customers that the firm has—in part because you made them that way.

Ongoing Training and Certification

Aside from an MBA, which you will likely need to advance beyond the associate level, private wealth management has little in the way of additional certifications and qualifications. Yes, you'll need your NASD Series exams, as described elsewhere in this book, but as a private banker, it's your hands-on experience that will serve as your education. Some firms may want their private bankers to have a CFA designation or other professional certifications, but others may simply see this as window dressing.

Most firms will have consistent ongoing training for analysts, associates and even vice presidents. There will be constant opportunities to talk to the firm's experts or even outside experts on the latest investment vehicles and opportunities. And the firm's monthly or quarterly investment outlook call or conference attracts almost universal firm attendance. There are refresher seminars before tax season so that private bankers are aware of the latest changes to the tax code, and portfolio planning strategy sessions on a regular basis.

If your private wealth management firm is connected to a larger bank or investment house, you'll be encouraged to take advantage of all the internal courses and seminars the larger company has to offer. Outside courses given by the Securities Industry Association or other trade groups may also be offered to you.

Should you find your talents skewing toward a particular specialty, such as fixed income investments or real estate transactions, your firm may sponsor additional training for you to help formalize your growing expertise.

Changing Careers Out of Private Wealth

There may very well come a day when you want out. It may stem from a frustration with private wealth management itself, a simple desire to try something new, pursuit of more money or expertise in a given area, or even a geographic change. Thankfully, the skills you'll develop in private wealth management can lead to a variety of other jobs in the financial industry.

If money's the object, you may want to move into more traditional sales and trading work, which is far more commission-driven. You may have to start a few steps behind someone of your age and experience, but not by much.

If your experiences have led you to some expertise in portfolio strategy, real estate transactions, fixed income or alternative investments, you may want to build on that knowledge, formalizing it with more graduate work or certifications, and then moving to an asset management firm, hedge fund or investment bank.

Never discount the customer service skills you've accumulated through the years. Many financial institutions are becoming far more attuned to the needs of the customer, and if you've received some management experience along the way, you could find yourself heading up the service arm of a major financial firm.

There's also academia for those tired of the rat race. Business schools, both undergraduate and graduate, look to improve their expertise in private wealth management as the industry grows. Your MBA and work experience could be enough to get you a slot at a grad school teaching portfolio theory, while a few years getting your PhD could mean a fulfilling second career as a full-time professor, working at the cutting edge of investment thinking.

You can also split off and form your own private wealth management firm. There are high-net-worth individuals out there who prefer a more personal approach to their banking, and may feel that the Citigroups, Merrill Lynches or Credit Suisses of the world aren't giving them the attention they deserve. While you won't be able to poach from your firm, you'll certainly have the contacts and resources available to hunt down new clients. You'll need to work heavily on your infrastructure before you start, however, since high-net-worth clients expect a certain amount of professionalism—no running your firm out of your home office!

Visit the Vault Finance Career Channel at **www.vault.com/finance** – with insider firm profiles, message boards, the Vault Finance Job Board and more.

VAULT CAREER LIBRARY

85

You'll also need to develop relationships with independent lawyers, accountants, lenders, brokerages and real estate experts to make up for the holes in your own areas of expertise. This isn't necessarily a bad thing, however, as these experts can also drive customers to your door just as much as you bring business to them.

Plus, you'll have to put your clients' money somewhere! The nice thing about being a solo advisor is that you choose investment opportunities available from several firms rather than focusing on products available only to the clients of those big firms. You can have a Chase money market, a Fidelity brokerage and a variety of mutual fund or hedge fund investments, for example—whatever is best suited to the clients' needs.

Alternatively, you may be asked by a client to run his or her family office. Reserved for the ultra-high-net-worth individuals, family offices take on all the financial responsibilities of extremely wealthy families that are practically an institution themselves. A family office manages the family fortune, and in some cases oversees businesses that the family owns. In many cases, the family office makes sure each member of the family receives his or her "allowance" and ensures that homes, loans and bills are all taken care of, and that any staff employed by the family is paid. Some family offices are small, one-person operations, while others can seem like a full private wealth management team, with accountants, investment gurus and other specialists working together for a single family and its wealth.

Lifestyle

CHAPTER 10

Lifestyle Considerations

Hours

There are no 9-to-5 jobs on Wall Street, and private wealth management is no exception. With the evolving 24/7 nature of the marketplace and the increasing diversity and popularity of global investment products, private bankers have to keep abreast of their clients' holdings all the time, and be ready to act at a moment's notice. If the Hong Kong market melts down in the middle of the night, the banker better be ready in the morning to tell his client exactly how he handled the crisis overnight.

That said, private bankers say their hours tend to be better than those of their colleagues in investment banking or asset management. Crises like the one described above happen infrequently at most, and the majority of private banking clients tend to invest in safer vehicles that require less monitoring, at least outside business hours. "I definitely put in my hours, and my clients know they can call me any time they want," says one private banker. "But for the most part, when I leave for the weekend, the weekend is mine."

That same banker, however, reports taking a BlackBerry and laptop—with wide-area wireless Internet access card—on every vacation, no matter how short or long. These, however, are rarely, if ever, used while away.

Of course, the exceptions to the rules make life interesting. Private bankers report having weekends cut short by all kinds of issues and requests. One banker had to find a way to get cash to a client who had lost his wallet while hiking in a remote part of Europe, while another flew out to Miami early on a Sunday morning to help a client who, on the spur of the moment, decided to purchase a stake in the nightclub he had enjoyed the previous evening.

Few bankers report real "crunch time" experiences like the ones that always seem to crop up in, say, investment banking. There will be times, certainly, when the acquisition of a home, the settlement of a divorce case or various contracts and loan provisions could keep a banker up late. Still, with preservation of capital the hallmark of private banking, most bankers can put

Visit the Vault Finance Career Channel at **www.vault.com/finance** – with insider firm profiles, message boards, the Vault Finance Job Board and more.

VAULT CAREER LIBRARY   87

in a full day's work, usually 10 to 12 hours, and then head home with the expectation that the evening or weekend is theirs.

Stress on the job

Stress and finance careers go together, it seems, and while a private banker may not experience the stress of putting together a multibillion-dollar merger, or feel the tension in the "boiler room" during a market downturn, there's still plenty of things that can make for a bad day.

Deadline stress is almost universal on Wall Street, and private wealth management is no exception. You may end up working long hours against a tight deadline to secure a line of credit for a client, or close on a real estate investment. Tax time is another headache. And as your client goes through personal crises, whether it's divorce or the loss of a loved one, you'll be taking on the financial stresses to help alleviate your client's personal stress.

Having the marketplace prove you wrong is another universal problem that crops up in private wealth management. As anybody with an interest in the markets can tell you, they can turn on you at any time, with the best laid plans and strategies flushed on a moment's notice. It's relatively rare, but it does and will happen. You will indeed make a bad decision with regard to your client's money at some point, even if it's because of some event in the marketplace that nobody could foresee. You'll have to answer to your client when that happens—never a pleasant prospect.

And of course, the clients themselves can often be a source of stress that's unique to private wealth management. "I have one client that, I swear, has to be convinced of every single thing I bring to her, even if it's the simplest, easiest and most practical thing you could think of," one small-firm private banker says. "I spent two hours once trying to convince her that a certificate of deposit was about as risk free as you can get in investing."

Clients are people, and people sometimes do irrational things that make private bankers want to scream. Even the most intelligent, sophisticated client can end up disagreeing with you on the best way to manage his money, and you must ultimately abide by the client's wishes, even if you feel strongly that it's not a good idea. And there are certainly clients who will want to talk every time the market makes a blip lower (though not higher, usually), panicked about investment decisions. "Talking down" clients can become a big part of your day, depending on your client base.

And while most private wealth management clients are generally financially savvy in their own right, there are those who will need lots of extra attention for even the most innocuous moves with their money. Some people are simply naturally cautious, or have been bitten by bad investments in the past, and need some coddling and hand-holding. It's emotionally draining, but it is part of the job, regardless, and the bonus money or commission is generally worth the hassle.

Diversity

There's no real measurement or survey work done on ethnic diversity in the private wealth management industry, and most private banks say it's still a primarily white male establishment, catering primarily to other white males and their families. That said, high-net-worth clients are slowly becoming more diverse themselves, and a number of major companies, most notably Merrill Lynch & Co., are targeting minority clients who are starting to approach high-net-worth status.

The vast majority of Wall Street firms have diversity programs in place to attract women and minorities, and that goes for their private wealth management divisions as well. Firms are generally very hesitant to discuss the nature of their programs, their successes or failures, or any statistics involved, and probably with good reason. As one HR person says, "No matter how good you think you're doing, someone else is going to think it's mediocre, and someone else is going to think it's atrocious."

Some firms are quietly stocking up on minorities in hopes of going after minority clients. At least one private wealth management firm attached to a major investment bank has executives, themselves minorities, going out to attract newly wealthy minorities. "Nobody wants to be seen as 'targeting,' because there's negativity associated with that," one executive says. "Minorities have been ignored far too long in this country, and some find it objectionable to be catered to only when they're wealthy. And they have a point. Maybe we didn't give them a business loan 25 years ago. And now we want to manage their wealth from that business? Where were we then? It's a fine line." For now, however, private banking clients, and the private bankers who serve them, still skew white male.

Travel

Most of your clients will be based in the city where you keep your office, so for most private bankers, there's not a lot of travel. However, many high-net-worth individuals have second (or more) homes, and enjoy travel themselves.

Visit the Vault Finance Career Channel at **www.vault.com/finance** – with
insider firm profiles, message boards, the Vault Finance Job Board and more.

VAULT CAREER LIBRARY

89

In rare cases, you may be asked to meet with them somewhere else to discuss a pending investment or venture, or simply take a trip out to the Hamptons to discuss their quarterly statement rather than having them stop by your office.

You may also end up traveling to investigate a potential investment on behalf of your client. If you have a client that wants to start flipping condos in Miami, you may end up down there for a first-hand look—which could also help other clients on your client list and throughout your private wealth management firm. If there's a potential for firmwide benefit, your company will readily pay the bill. Otherwise, depending on where you work, you may end up charging your client for the travel, or you may just swallow the cost yourself if you feel it's necessary.

Also, a client based in your city may retire and move somewhere else, but will still keep you on board as his personal wealth manager. In that case, if the client is worth enough to your company, you very well may visit that client regularly.

Finally, in extremely rare cases, you may be asked to fly somewhere on a moment's notice to help a client with a financial or personal crisis. While unconfirmed, most private bankers say they've heard of colleagues who have had to head out in the middle of the night with bail money.

"It's like the really dirty jokes comedians tell each other when they're off stage," a Chicago private bank investment strategist says. "You hear all these stories about how somebody had to fly to Thailand to get a client's kid out of prison or you end up going on tour with a rock band for a week while trying to finish up a philanthropy deal. But then you ask around, and nobody actually knows the guy who went and did that stuff."

Your paycheck

As discussed earlier in this guide, analysts can start off with as little as $60,000 per year in salary and bonuses, while associates can expect $80,000 to $95,000 a year in salary and bonuses or commission their first year or two of handling clients. That number can grow steadily, however, as you gain new clients and help your current clients grow their portfolios and invest their hard-earned wealth.

Five years into your job as an associate, you can expect to make around $500,000 per year or more, most of it coming from bonuses or commissions rather than salary. In 10 to 15 years, that can reach at least $1 million per year. The top performing private bankers can exceed $3 million per year, and are usually at the vice president or managing director level.

Compared to the average run-of-the-mill job, this is exceptional. Compared to other jobs on Wall Street, however, it can seem about average. However, "there's just a lot more to private banking jobs than other jobs on Wall Street," says one banker. "The relationships you can build, the philanthropy you can help direct, the families you serve—these are pretty fulfilling. And I'm really quite happy with how I'm paid."

Uppers and Downers

Like any job, there are pros and cons to a career in private wealth management. The vast majority of private bankers are quite content in their jobs—but then again, they wouldn't be there if they weren't. Here are some uppers and downers that private bankers experience every day.

Uppers

• **Clients.** You'll be helping people realize their hopes and dreams, manage the results of a lifetime of hard work and plan for their futures. They're generally interesting people with fascinating life experiences, and you may end up becoming very close to them.

• **Entrepreneurship.** Once you're an associate or higher, you'll be ultimately responsible for your clients' performance, and you'll have the opportunity to build your own client base. You'll have quite a bit of input into how much money you make, based on your drive and your investment savvy.

• **On-the-job knowledge**. It's not just stocks and bonds. While you'll have backing from experts or consultants made available to you by your firm, you'll end up learning quite a bit about a variety of investments and financial planning tools. From real estate to hedge funds, from prenups to estate planning, you'll only get smarter as time goes on.

• **Philanthropy**. Many private bankers find particular joy from helping their clients give their money away. While it's not a high-commission activity by any stretch, it's certainly good for the soul. And as one banker pointed out, it can lead to more business contacts and potential clients!

Visit the Vault Finance Career Channel at **www.vault.com/finance** – with insider firm profiles, message boards, the Vault Finance Job Board and more.

VAULT CAREER LIBRARY

91

- **Lifestyle.** For the most part, you can actually have a life outside of work if you manage your time and client accounts properly. You won't have many eight-hour days, but you can reasonably expect to have weekends free, and you'll be able to take vacations like the rest of humanity.

- **Money**. While you'll never receive multimillion-dollar checks for leading a merger deal, you'll certainly be making plenty of money, enough to easily become a high-net-worth individual in your own right.

Downers

- **Clients**. While the majority of your clients will fall into the "uppers" category, a few will most certainly drive you nuts. They'll ignore your advice, do stupid things with their money, and then blame you for it. A few will call constantly with each tick of the market, and some will need hand-holding or supremely well-thought-out arguments for each move you think they should make. Even your best clients will make you want to pull your hair out every now and again.

- **Conservatism.** Many of your clients will be risk adverse, and investments that could make them (and you) a pretty penny could be summarily rejected despite your best arguments.

- **Income fluctuations.** Feeding into the above, you may end up having a run of low bonuses or commissions due to uncertainty in the markets or a conservative investing trend. Just as your clients can fall prey to the vagaries of the market, your own income will as well.

- **Always on.** While the majority of your clients will leave you alone on weekends, holidays and vacations, you'll constantly have to be ready to spring into action at a moment's notice. Don't think of even heading to the grocery store without your BlackBerry on, and if you're going on vacation, a laptop with a reliable wireless connection is essential. An understanding domestic partner is also important should a client call in the middle of a honeymoon or family holiday.

• **Limited geographic potential**. You're going to have to live where high-net-worth individuals live, which means a major U.S. or world city, with all the expense and headaches that come along with it. You can certainly live in the suburbs, but if you're hankering for a small-town lifestyle, you won't get it—at least not without a major commute.

Visit the Vault Finance Career Channel at **www.vault.com/finance** – with
insider firm profiles, message boards, the Vault Finance Job Board and more.

VAULT CAREER LIBRARY   93

PRIVATE WEALTH MANAGEMENT FIRM PROFILES

The Private Bank of Bank of America

One Federal Street
Boston, MA 02110
Phone: (617) 346-4477
Fax: (617) 346-4520
www.bankofamerica.com

EMPLOYMENT CONTACT

Stephanie Davidson
E-mail: stephanie.davidson@
bankofamerica.com
Phone: (704) 895-5894
www.bankofamerica.com/care
ers

Chairman & CEO: Ken Lewis
Firm Type: Public Company
2005 Private Wealth Management Revenue (Worldwide): $2 billion
2005 Total Firm Revenue (Worldwide): $56.9 billion
2005 Total Firm Net Income (Worldwide): $16.5 billion
No. of Employees (Private Wealth): 2,000
No. of Employees (GWIM): 12,500
No. of Office Locations (Worldwide): 150

Hiring Process

In addition to campuses, where else does your firm recruit for employees?

On the firm's web site, interested candidates can create a profile and submit a resume to be considered for opportunities. Through the career page, candidates can search open positions by job family or location.

Please describe your summer internships.

The intern program typically begins in May and continues through September. Our application deadline is mid-February each year. We usually fill positions by mid-April.

Bank of America offers paid internships. Candidates must have an overall GPA of 3.0 or above and be enrolled full time in an undergraduate or graduate program at an accredited college. Interns must be eligible to work 40 hours per week for the program length of 10 to 12 weeks and must be pursuing a major in a business or technical-related area. Candidates must have work status in the U.S., as it is not the practice of Bank of America to sponsor individuals for work visas.

Inside the Firm: Culture and Training

Please describe the corporate culture at your firm.

The following five values represent what we believe in as individuals and as a team, and how we aspire to interact with our customers, our shareholders, our communities and one another. Our five core values are: Doing the right thing, trusting and teamwork, inclusive meritocracy, winning and leadership.

Please describe any scholarship programs at your firm.

The tuition reimbursement program helps employees pay for college tuition and tuition-related expenses to make it easier to pursue educational goals. Employees may request reimbursement up to the maximum amount allowed each calendar year with no limit on the number of course(s) credit hours taken. For eligible undergraduate courses, reimbursement up to $2,000 each calendar year is available. (Your reimbursement is considered non-taxable income.) For eligible graduate courses, you may be reimbursed up to $4,000 each calendar year. The program is open to U.S.-based associates who are actively employed at the time the course begins and remain employed at the time of reimbursement. Courses through an accredited college or university as published by the American Council on Education are eligible. The course does not have to be job or business-related and associate does not have to be completing a degree.

Compensation

Please describe compensation at your firm.

In addition to strong base compensation, bonuses and incentive programs are important parts of our overall compensation package. Employees can take advantage of a 401(k) plan and funded pension plan. Shortly after you start work, you can begin contributing up to 30 percent of pay on a before-tax basis to a 401(k) plan. After one year of service, Bank of America matches your contribution up to 5 percent of pay. After one year of service, each month Bank of America adds to your pension account, which grows as the investment gains over time. When you leave the company, you can receive your vested benefits in a lump sum if you choose.

Please describe other perks.

Eligible employees can take advantage of discounts on a wide range of bank services, from checking accounts to credit cards. In addition, to honor associates who volunteer their time and service to causes important to them, the Bank of America

Charitable Foundation awards grants (up to $500 per person each calendar year), donated in associates' names, to nonprofit organizations.

Diversity

Please describe any diversity hiring efforts in regards to women.

The firm recruits at a number of women's events, such as the Society of Women Engineers and National Women MBA Association. A full calendar is on the firm's career web site.

Please describe any diversity hiring efforts in regards to minorities.

Bank of America partners with national multicultural professional associations to recruit new talent and develop new business relationships. The firm is one of the largest corporate sponsors of the National Association of Black Accountants and of national African-American and Hispanic MBA organizations. Bank of America recruits at many events held by these associations, including those hosted by the National Society of Black Engineers, Association of Latino Professionals in Finance and Accounting and the National Asian Pacific American Bar Association. A calendar of events is maintained on the firm's career web site.

In addition to recruiting efforts, the bank has affinity groups (informal, company-recognized groups of associates with common interests) that meet periodically to network and support one another's development and success.

Additional Information

For more than 150 years, The Private Bank has been the advisor of choice for the affluent. Our experience is among the reasons that we've grown to be the nation's largest trustee for individuals, families and private foundations. The Private Bank offers expertise across a wide range of wealth management disciplines. The firm's specialists have the knowledge and training to guide clients in tax and retirement planning, trusts and wealth transfer, credit solutions, investment management and everyday banking.

Bank of America is one of the largest banks in the U.S.—with more than $100 billion in assets under management, a loan portfolio in excess of $22 billion and responsibility for billions more in oil, gas, farm, ranch and timberland properties. That broad scope of resources means we know how to meet you and your family's wealth management needs.

Visit the Vault Finance Career Channel at **www.vault.com/finance** — with insider firm profiles, message boards, the Vault Finance Job Board and more.

VAULT CAREER LIBRARY

99

The Private Bank of The Bank of New York

1 Wall Street New York, NY 10286 Phone: (212) 495-1784 Fax: (212) 809-9528 E-mail: info@bankofny.com www.bankofny.com **EMPLOYMENT CONTACT** See "careers" at www.bankofny.com	**Chairman & CEO:** Thomas A. Renyi **Firm Type:** Public Company **2005 Private Wealth Management Revenue (Worldwide):** $490 million **2005 Total Firm Revenue (Worldwide):** $6.8 billion **2005 Total Firm Net Income (Worldwide):** $1.57 billion **No. of Employees (Firmwide):** 23,451 **No. of Office Locations (Worldwide):** 342

Hiring Process

Recruiting

The firm recruits on college campuses; an updated recruiting calendar can be found on the career page of the web site.

In addition to campuses, where else does your firm recruit for employees?

Candidates are invited to create a profile with a resume and cover letter for the firm's searchable online database. The profile can be saved and used to apply directly to jobs posted on the web site. BNY Resourcing is the group responsible for screening, preselection and testing of candidates who apply for positions at the firm. After applying to The Bank of New York a BNY Resourcing consultant will contact select applicants to discuss the application in depth, answer questions about opportunities and prepare candidates for the interview process.

Visit Vault at **www.vault.com** for insider company profiles, expert advice, career message boards, expert resume reviews, the Vault Job Board and more.

VAULT CAREER LIBRARY   **101**

Hiring

What are the position titles for new hires coming out of undergrad? Out of grad school?

Associate.

Inside the Firm: Culture and Training

Please describe any scholarship programs at your firm.

The firm's tuition assistance program offers reimbursement for career-related college courses.

Compensation

Please describe other perks.

Employees receive a free checking account, free safety deposit box preferential rates on consumer loans and mortgages after one year of employment.

Diversity

Please describe any diversity hiring efforts in regards to minorities.

Bank of New York recruits through sources that promote the hiring of minorities, women and the disabled. Such sources include, INROADS; historically black colleges such as Howard, Spelman and Morehouse; the Financial Women's Association; and the International Center for the Disabled. The firm also participates in various MBA minority career fairs such as the Black Business Students Association at Columbia University, the Association of Hispanic and Black Business Students at New York University, the Whitney M. Young, Jr. Memorial Conference at Wharton, the Consortium for Graduate Study in Management and the Urban Bankers' Coalition of New York career fair. The firm is also active in recruiting with the National Black MBA Association, NYC chapter.

Additional Information

Since 1784, The Private Bank of the Bank of New York has served clients in areas such as estate planning, trusts, custody, investment management and custom financing to help clients successfully achieve financial goals.

Barclays Private Bank

200 Park Avenue
New York, NY 10166
Phone: (212) 412-4000
E-mail: info@barclays.com
www.barclays.com

EMPLOYMENT CONTACT

www.barclays.co.uk/careers/

Chairman: Matthew W. Barrett
CEO: John Varley
Firm Type: Public Company
2005 Private Wealth Management Revenue (Worldwide): £928 million
2005 Total Firm Revenue (Worldwide): £17.97 billion
2005 Total Firm Net Income (Worldwide): £15.76 billion
No. of Employees (Private Wealth): 7,200
No. of Employees (Firmwide): 118,000
No. of Office Locations (Worldwide): 32

Hiring Process

Recruiting

The firm recruits from undergraduate and graduate programs at college campuses worldwide. A current recruiting calendar is maintained on the Global Events page of the firm's web site. Candidates can also search for jobs online and apply through the firm's web site.

Hiring

The way candidates are selected depends on the type of role sought, but will generally consist of an interview and one or two practical exercises. Candidates need to show an understanding of what is required in the role, as well as being able to discuss why they want to do it. And, for the practical exercises, candidates may be asked to do something in a group. Information about recruiting can be found on the firm's web site.

What are some of the requirements for jobs?

We offer many career opportunities for those with an excellent academic background coupled with a creative and imaginative mind.

Please describe your summer internships.

Summer internships are offered for candidates in their final two years of study. Internships begin in June and last 10 to 12 weeks. Candidates should submit applications online through the web site.

Inside the Firm: Culture and Training

Please describe any mentoring programs at your firm.

All new hires are given access to the online graduate mentoring program. The system allows individuals to select a suitable mentor to help them integrate into the firm as well as to gain a sound understanding of the firm's structure, values and expectations.

Please describe any formal training programs for employees.

New hires have the opportunity to participate in the Barclays Capital Global Campus Training Programme. Global Campus is the firm's web-based training program that focuses on product education and covers both credit and rates modules. It is designed to give new hires a thorough knowledge of the firm's products prior to joining the Graduate Programme.

Compensation

Please describe compensation and other monetary benefits at your firm.

An annual discretionary bonus is given based on individual and firm performance.

The firm offers employees a 20 percent discount on the price of Barclays shares through monthly savings plans, Sharepurchase and Sharesave. Other benefits include a pension plan, child care savings program and reduced rate loans.

Please describe other perks.

Employees are eligible for discounts on auto purchases, gym memberships, home computers and theater and concert tickets.

Diversity

Please describe any diversity hiring efforts in regards to minorities.

Diversity is a business imperative and the firm is committed to being an organization that values diversity and promotes the inclusion of all people who share the firm's aspirations and performance expectations.

Please describe any diversity hiring efforts in regards to gays and lesbians.

Aside from hiring initiatives, the firm has several diversity-focused employee networks: Cultural Diversity for employees from ethnic minorities, Pos+Ability for colleagues with disabilities and Spectrum for gay, lesbian, bisexual and transgender employees. These groups give all employees the opportunity to explore their interests and develop their understanding of diversity issues.

Additional Information

Barclay's wealth management products and services are tailored to meet the specific needs of clients with a minimum of £500,000 (or currency equivalent) in investable assets. The firm assists with day-to-day investment management, maximizing clients' tax efficiency and developing the financial awareness of younger family members.

The wealth management division serves clients through wealth structuring, investment management, banking and credit solutions.

Visit the Vault Finance Career Channel at **www.vault.com/finance** — with
insider firm profiles, message boards, the Vault Finance Job Board and more.

VAULT CAREER LIBRARY   **105**

Bear Stearns Private Client Services

383 Madison Ave.
New York, NY 10179
Phone: (212) 272-2000
Fax: (212) 272-7038
www.bearstearns.com

EMPLOYMENT CONTACT

Career web site address:
See the "careers" page at
www.bearstearns.com

Firm Chairman & CEO: James E. Cayne
Firm Type: Public Company
2005 Private Wealth Management Revenue (Worldwide): $450.2 million
2005 Total Firm Net Revenue (Worldwide): $7.4 billion
2005 Total Firm Net Income (Worldwide): $1.5 billion
No. of Employees (Private Wealth): 500
No. of Employees (Firmwide): 12,500
No. of Office Locations (Worldwide): Offices in 19 cities

Hiring Process

Recruiting

The firm conducts campus recruiting; candidates should check with the career services office at their campus to sign up for an interview. If we do not visit your campus, we will review your online resume and contact you by the end of October if your background matches an open position. Candidates selected for interviews will be notified via e-mail.

In addition to campuses, where else does your firm recruit for employees?

Candidates are invited to submit a resume through the career page of the web site.

Visit Vault at **www.vault.com** for insider company profiles, expert advice, career message boards, expert resume reviews, the Vault Job Board and more.

VAULT CAREER LIBRARY   107

Hiring

What are the position titles for new hires coming out of undergrad? Out of grad school?

New hires coming out of undergrad can enter the private client services division as a sales assistant trainee. As a trainee, you'll work with a mentor during your introduction to the brokerage industry and have an opportunity to earn your Series 7 license. The Bear Stearns account executives who will guide you are among the most knowledgeable and successful on the Street. Our client-driven firm consistently attracts sales assistants who thrive on the daily challenges presented by the PCS division and its fast pace. With hard work and persistence, you'll realize the learning never stops. You'll enjoy the rewards of using practical knowledge provided by a supportive mentor.

Please describe the hiring process at your firm.

If the firm's recruiters do not visit your campus, we will review your online resume and contact you by the end of October if your background matches an open position. Candidates selected for interviews will be notified via e-mail. A list of interview prep strategies is on the career page of the web site.

What are some of the requirements for jobs?

For the private client services sales assistant position, the firm seeks highly motivated candidates who have a bachelor's degree (preferably in business), brokerage industry experience, and superior oral and written communication skills. Given the international nature of our business, foreign language skills can be a plus. Candidates with Series 7 and 63 licenses are preferred.

For the private client services sales assistant trainee position, the firm looks for diligent self-starters who have a bachelor's degree (ideally in business), an excellent academic record, superior oral and written communication skills and the ability to work well in fast-paced environments.

Inside the Firm: Culture and Training

Please describe the corporate culture at your firm.

Bear Stearns' culture rewards innovative thinking and gives its employees the resources to succeed. The cornerstones of our culture are accessibility, flexibility, entrepreneurialism and visibility. The four cultural characteristics discussed above create extraordinary opportunities for professional growth and development. The process begins on your first day with Bear Stearns and continues as you pursue your career at the firm. Along the way, you will benefit from the leadership of experienced, motivated and talented professionals. We will empower you with the specific skills and tools you need to build a solid foundation and fully utilize your potential.

The success and stability of Bear Stearns can be attributed to its people. Our employees take pride in their work and ownership of their careers. To learn more about the opportunities at Bear Stearns and decide which one may be best for you, please visit the web site. You will find perspectives on what it is like to work at one of Wall Street's most innovative and prestigious firms.

Compensation

Please describe compensation and other monetary benefits at your firm.

Some employees are eligible for a performance-oriented bonus in addition to base salary.

The firm offers 401(k) and profit-sharing plans for employees.

Please describe other perks.

A variety of special services and corporate discounts are available to employees.

Diversity

Please describe any diversity hiring efforts in regards to women.

The firm recruits at women's career fairs and events, such as the National Association of Women MBAs and the Women for Hire Career Fair.

Please describe any diversity hiring efforts in regards to minorities.

The firm is involved with The Consortium for Graduate Study in Management, a nonprofit group of 14 graduate business schools dedicated to providing management education opportunities to Native Americans and other minorities seeking business careers. Bear Stearns holds recruiting events at a number of conferences, such as the Black Business Students Association Conference (BBSA), African-American Business Association/ Hispanic American Business Students Diversity Career Fair, Asian Diversity Career Fair and the National Society of Hispanic MBAs.

Visit the Vault Finance Career Channel at **www.vault.com/finance** — with
insider firm profiles, message boards, the Vault Finance Job Board and more.

V/\ULT CAREER LIBRARY

109

Additional Information

Bear Stearns' private client services division (PCS) is a leader in servicing high-net-worth individuals, money managers, and small corporations. Our individual clients derive important benefits normally reserved for institutional clients at other Wall Street firms. They enjoy unparalleled access to experts from all areas of the firm, and benefit from the leverage afforded by Bear Stearns' capital strength and its trading and underwriting expertise.

The firm's unique client-driven culture continues to attract Wall Street's most talented investment professionals. We maintain our sales force at an optimal size for providing superior client service. A select group of approximately 500 account executives works within a network of eight domestic branch offices. The exclusive nature of PCS enables us to provide our clients with prompt access to research analysts, traders, investment bankers and members of senior management.

In addition to direct investments in equity and fixed income products, we offer clients a wide selection of alternative investment opportunities. Our performance-driven culture fosters the creative thinking that enables us to offer clients options they would not have access to on their own, such as leveraged buyout funds, venture capital funds and private equity funds. Today, more than ever, our clients are turning to us for sophisticated investment strategies. In response, we offer some of the most innovative products on Wall Street.

Brown Brothers Harriman
Private Wealth Management

140 Broadway
New York, NY 10005-1101
Phone: (212) 483-1818
Fax: (212) 493-7287
www.bbh.com

McConnell
Firm Type: Private Company
No. of Employees (Firmwide):
2,800
**No. of Office Locations
(Worldwide):** 15

EMPLOYMENT
CONTACT

E-mail: jobs@bbh.com
Fax: (212) 493-7287
www.bbh.com/career/index.htm
Managing Partner: Michael W.

Hiring Process

Recruiting

The firm conducts on-campus recruiting at various schools, including Harvard, Dartmouth, Williams College and Connecticut College.

Where else does your firm recruit for employees?

Candidates can search job opportunities and submit a resume and profile directly through the firm's web site.

Hiring

Please describe the hiring process at your firm.

The interview process typically begins with a telephone interview, followed by one or more days of on-site meetings with our recruiters and members of management. There is no established time frame for the recruiting process; it lasts long enough for the firm and candidate to learn enough about each other to make an informed decision.

Visit Vault at **www.vault.com** for insider company profiles, expert advice, career message boards, expert resume reviews, the Vault Job Board and more.

VAULT CAREER LIBRARY   111

Inside the Firm: Culture and Training

Please describe the corporate culture at your firm.

Our employees are expected to think fast and work hard. Our culture is driven by strong values-we encourage employees to nurture their community and family lives as well as their professional performance. By getting involved in our BBHcares program, employees can be a part of the firm's commitment to social responsibility. Through our many work/life balance initiatives, we provide ways to balance career and personal life.

Please describe any mentoring programs at your firm.

BBH's self-directed approach to mentoring provides employees with information and resources to help them serve as mentors or partners with mentors to learn and grow in their careers.

Please describe any scholarship programs at your firm.

The firm offers tuition reimbursement up to $8,000 a year for up to two classes a semester, or eight classes per year.

Please describe any formal training programs for employees.

All new employees participate in a general orientation process called BBHConnections/My First Year. Additionally, some areas of the firm offer formal training programs, but all provide valuable on-the-job training. BBH also partners with employees (through mentoring programs, supplemental training courses and regular feedback) to address their long-term career development needs.

Please describe any ongoing or other training programs for employees.

The firm's dedicated global training & development (GT&D) team will support employees' educational needs throughout their career at BBH. From the classroom to Intranet-based training at your desktop, GT&D offers a variety of courses for personal and career growth.

Developing My Career is a program that provides employees with resources and guidance to help define where they are in their careers, where they want to go and steps to take to reach their goals.

Compensation

Please describe compensation and other monetary benefits at your firm.

In addition to performance bonuses, BBH offers a defined benefit pension plan, fully paid by the firm, and a partially matched 401(k) plan. Employees are also eligible for flexible spending health and commuting accounts, a brokerage discount with Charles Schwab, mortgage assistance services and discounts at various partner companies. After employees have completed two years of continuous employment, their children are eligible to apply for financial scholarships, based on academic achievement, for their college education through the Undergraduate Fund.

Citigroup Private Bank

Address: 399 Park Avenue New York, NY 10043 Phone: (212) 559-1000 Fax: (212) 793-3946 www.citigroup.com **EMPLOYMENT CONTACT** General career site: See "careers" at www.citigroup.com Citigroup Private Bank career web site address: www.citibank.com/privatebank/ careers.htm	**Firm Chairman & CEO:** Charles (Chuck) Prince **Firm Type:** Public Company **2005 Private Wealth Management Revenue (Worldwide):** $373 million **2005 Total Firm Revenue (Worldwide):** $86.3 billion **2005 Total Firm Net Income (Worldwide):** $24.6 billion **No. of Employees (Private Wealth):** 3,955 **No. of Employees (Firmwide):** 275,000 **No. of Office Locations (Worldwide):** 7,500

Hiring Process

Recruiting

On the Career Center page of the firm's web site, an updated list of campus recruiting events is made available before the start of the school year. Candidates are invited to search for jobs and submit a profile online through the career page.

Hiring

What are the position titles for new hires coming out of undergrad? Out of grad school?

For new hires coming out of undergrad, Citigroup Private Bank's analyst program develops the skills required to become a member of a product or sales team within the private bank. The three-year program provides analysts with varied business experiences within product and/or sales teams. Roles are determined by business need, and analysts have the opportunity of rotating throughout the following areas: banker teams, investment management and capital markets.

Analysts perform a wide range of tasks that vary depending upon which team they work in. Responsibilities may include developing financial models, helping to evaluate investment ideas for clients, preparing presentations for client visits and helping to develop new client business. Initial training and placements are in New York. Opportunities in other U.S. offices (San Francisco, Los Angeles and Chicago) are available on an individual and business need basis. Each year, a select number of third-year analysts will be invited to join Citigroup Private Bank's associate program.

Graduate students who are new hires enter the associate program at the Citigroup Private Bank. The associate program develops the skills required to become a member of a product or sales team within the private bank. Roles are determined by matching specific business needs and individual skill sets. Associates join one of the following teams: banker teams, investment management, capital markets or business strategy. Associates perform a wide range of tasks that vary depending upon which team they work with. Responsibilities may include developing new client relationships, helping to create and implementing wealth management strategies for clients, and developing and presenting investment proposals.

Please describe the hiring process at your firm.

The private bank's recruitment process involves two interviews with senior managers. Each interview will assess the applicant's skills and potential within the dynamic private banking industry. Successful applicants are invited to our New York offices to learn more about the firm and the opportunities available.

What are some of the requirements for jobs?

Analysts within the private bank have a combination of strong analytical and interpersonal skills. Individuals need to be self-motivated, good team players and possess excellent written and verbal communication skills. A demonstrated interest in the financial services industry is essential. In addition to these skills, applicants should be current seniors in an undergraduate program and maintain a minimum 3.0 GPA.

Associates within the Private Bank have a combination of strong analytical and interpersonal skills. Individuals need to be self-motivated, good team players and possess excellent written and verbal communication skills. A demonstrated interest in the financial services industry is essential.

Please describe your summer internships.

Citigroup Private Bank's summer associate program runs for 10 weeks. Open to MBA students, the program develops the skills required to become a member of a product or sales team within the private bank. Opportunities are available for summer associates to work on banker teams, in investment management, on the capital markets team or in business strategy. Summer associates perform a wide range of tasks that vary depending upon which team they work on. Responsibilities include developing new client relationships, helping to create wealth management strategies for clients and developing and presenting investment proposals. Summer associates within the private bank have a combination of strong analytical and interpersonal skills. Individuals need to be self-motivated, good team players and demonstrate excellent written and verbal communication skills.

Inside the Firm: Culture and Training

Please describe the corporate culture at your firm.

To support our growth as a leader in the private banking industry, Citigroup Private Bank employees are innovative, constantly thinking of new and better ways to service our clients and make our business an industry leader. A true meritocracy, Citigroup Private Bank recognizes and rewards achievement, collaboration and the highest standards of integrity. We are successful only when our clients have absolute confidence in our organization and our people, so our people take time to earn trust and build relationships with clients that will last for generations.

Please describe any formal training programs for employees.

For undergraduates entering the firm, Citigroup Private Bank's analyst training involves an intensive six-week program. Topics covered include investment management, capital markets, accounting, financial and tax statement analysis, and credit. During the course of the program, analysts work on several case studies and group projects. They also participate in discussions and presentations with senior management, gaining insights into the dynamic and competitive private banking industry. Continuing education is delivered on a monthly basis throughout the three-year program.

The associate training program is for new hires with a graduate degree. Training is approximately eight weeks in duration and provides the specific skills and knowledge needed to succeed at Citigroup Private Bank. Advanced training topics include investment management, capital markets, structured lending, trust and estate, selling

Visit the Vault Finance Career Channel at **www.vault.com/finance** — with insider firm profiles, message boards, the Vault Finance Job Board and more.

VAULT CAREER LIBRARY

117

and presentation skills, and prospecting. Classes are taught by a combination of world-class consultants, university professors and banking professionals. During the course of the program, associates will work on several case studies and group projects. They will also participate in discussions and presentations with senior management, gaining insights into the dynamic and competitive private banking industry. Following this initial program, continuing education is delivered on an ongoing basis.

Please describe any ongoing or other training programs for employees.

The ongoing development of our talent is a top priority for Citigroup Private Bank, and we provide progressive professional development curriculum to support our employee's efforts to expand their knowledge and improve their skills to reach higher levels of achievement. We recognize that successful development begins with an awareness of strengths and opportunities for improvement, and is realized through on-the-job experiences, learning from others and participating in relevant courses. All employees are encouraged to use feedback from their colleagues and take advantage of our comprehensive training offerings to create their own roadmap for their careers.

Diversity

Please describe any diversity hiring efforts in regards to women.

We continued to participate in professional diversity career fairs, including Women for Hire and the Urban Financial Services Coalition (UFSC). For example, we hired five women through Women for Hire, which brings the business community together with experienced female professionals in computer engineering, information technology, finance and marketing.

Please describe any diversity hiring efforts in regards to minorities.

To recruit the best talent, we strengthened partnerships with organizations such as the National Black MBA Association and the National Society of Hispanic MBAs. In 2003, Citigroup hired 17 MBAs from these two associations alone for management positions. We are also a member of both organizations' advisory boards and work closely with their national offices and local affiliates.

INROADS is another important partner. In 2003, through the INROADS program, 48 summer interns were hired and placed in various Citigroup businesses. Citigroup supports the Robert A. Toigo Foundation, an organization that provides fellowships for top minority students pursuing MBAs.

The firm partners with the Consortium for Graduate Studies in Management, an alliance of 18 leading U.S. business schools that help talented African-American, Hispanic American and Native American college graduates pursue careers in business. Citigroup sponsors the Consortium's orientation for new fellows and manages the Citigroup Ethics seminars in financial services and investment banking.

Please describe any diversity hiring efforts in regards to gays and lesbians.

Citigroup sponsors GLBT receptions at leading business schools; we also sponsored the 2003 Reaching Out MBA, Inc. conference in New York, which provides a forum for GLBT MBA candidates, recent business school alumni and business leaders to meet, share information and build networks.

Additional Information

Citigroup Private Bank serves the financial needs of more than 26,000 successful and influential individuals and families. Globally, the private bank has more than 3,955 employees, spanning 33 countries, and manages more than $203 billion in client business volume.

Our investment, banking and wealth advisory services are built upon three core capabilities: tailored lending services to address our clients' need for liquidity, capital markets solutions to help mitigate the risks of concentrated ownership positions and a wide spectrum of investment management strategies to help counterbalance the effects of highly correlated assets. Our private bankers draw on specialist teams, industry-leading innovations and proprietary technologies to meet our clients' specific wealth management needs.

Commerce Bank Private Banking

Commerce Atrium 1701 Route 70 East Cherry Hill, NJ 08034-5400 Phone: (856) 751-9000 Fax: (856) 751-9260 www.commerceonline.com **EMPLOYMENT** **CONTACT** Katrina Van Alstyne Phone: (856) 751-9000 www.commerceonline.com/ap ply_for_a_job/index.cfm	**Chairman & CEO:** Vernon W. Hill II **Firm Type:** Public Company **2005 Total Firm Revenue** **(Worldwide):** $1.69 billion **2005 Total Firm Net Income** **(Worldwide):** $282.9 million **No. of Employees (Firmwide):** 13,000 **No. of Office Locations** **(Worldwide):** 373

Hiring Process

Recruiting

The firm conducts on-campus recruiting at college campuses throughout the U.S. Contact the recruiting department for a campus recruiting calendar.

In addition to campuses, where else does your firm recruit for employees?

The bank lists opportunities on several job search web sites such as hotjobs.com and monster.com.

Hiring

What are some of the requirements for jobs?

The ideal candidate has strong leadership skills; excellent interpersonal, communication and problem-solving skills; and the drive to provide superior quality service to our customers. A bachelor's degree in a business related discipline is strongly preferred.

Inside the Firm: Culture and Training

Please describe any formal training programs for employees.

Commerce University is the bank's formal training facility made of five separate schools. Located in Mount Laurel, N.J., the training facility also has 16 satellite locations throughout Philadelphia, New York, Washington, D.C., and Southeast Florida. The university has a staff of 40 full-time educators and 100 adjunct instructors who provide a wide range of courses at the main campus and satellite locations. In the fall of 2006, the facility will move into a new 64,000-square-foot, state-of-the-art education and conference center in Mount Laurel. It offers one of the most extensive training and professional development programs in the financial services field and offers courses online, as well as on location.

Please describe any ongoing or other training programs for employees:

Commerce University offers a wide range of professional development classes for employees throughout their career.

Compensation

Please describe compensation and other monetary benefits at your firm.

The firm offers educational assistance for full- and part-time employees, a 401(k) with corporate match, discounts on home and auto insurance, discounted stock purchase plan with $500 in Commerce Bank stock, free banking services and various incentive programs.

Additional Information

Commerce private banking was only available in the New York Metro market until 2005, when the group expanded to provide services in Philadelphia, Washington D.C., and Southeast Florida.

Credit Suisse Private Banking

11 Madison Avenue
New York, NY 10010
Phone: (212) 325-2000
www.credit-suisse.com

EMPLOYMENT CONTACT

www.credit-suisse.com/standout

Private Banking CEO: Walter Berchtold
Credit Suisse CEO: Oswald J. Grübel
Firm Type: Public Company
2005 Private Wealth Management Pre-tax Income (Worldwide): $2.6 billion
2005 Total Firm Revenue (Worldwide): $49.3 billion
2005 Total Firm Net Income (Worldwide): $4.8 billion
No. of Employees (Firmwide): 63,040
No. of Office Locations (Private Banking USA): 9 offices in U.S.
No. of Office Locations (Worldwide): 70+

Hiring Process

Recruiting

See www.credit-suisse.com/standout for a list of colleges at which the firm recruits, along with a recruiting schedule. The firm recruits from Ivy League and other public and private institutions.

Hiring

What are the position titles for new hires coming out of undergrad? Out of grad school?

Undergrad: None; Grad: Summer Associate and Associate.

Please describe the hiring process at your firm.

Tips on applying and interviewing can be found at www.credit-suisse.com/standout.

What are some of the requirements for jobs?

Grads entering private banking must have an MBA or a JD. The firm is looking for results-oriented, entrepreneurial, motivated, flexible and creative candidates who have proven academic excellence, and have strong analytical skills and a capacity to grasp firmwide and market concepts.

Please describe your summer internships.

Summer associate internships are available for students entering their last year of grad school. Summer associate internships last nine to 10 weeks; interns are given junior and senior mentors. As a summer associate, you will work to support advisors, learning firsthand what managing the assets of some of the world's wealthiest individuals truly entails.

Inside the Firm: Culture and Training

Please describe the corporate culture at your firm.

Promising engrossing work and an energizing work environment, Credit Suisse looks for initiative in all of its employees, no matter how far down the ladder. Innovation and a willingness to immerse oneself in the work are rewarded here, with "no barriers to achievement." Credit Suisse boasts an "open-minded culture," emphasizing diversity of all kinds and mutual respect both within the firm and in the surrounding community.

Please describe any mentoring programs at your firm.

Full-time and summer associates will be assigned formal mentors who will provide advice and guidance.

Please describe any scholarship programs at your firm.

The MBA Explorer Program is a two-day educational outreach program that brings together students who are entering business school in the fall. In the past, the participants have been of diverse ethnic backgrounds, both male and female. In 2006, we targeted only female candidates. This unique program offers students who may not have an investment banking background a chance to learn firsthand about Wall Street and specifically Credit Suisse. Participants learn about the firm's core businesses and culture, and meet with school teams and recruiters months in advance of the summer associate recruiting season.

Please describe any ongoing or other training programs for employees.

The Credit Suisse Business School provides courses and programs for both management and specialist employees "that correspond to their function within the company as well as their training requirements."

Diversity

Please describe any diversity hiring efforts in regards to minorities.

Credit Suisse's Global Dignity at Work policy governs both the employing practices and the everyday operations of their offices all over the world. The policy makes it the responsibility of each employee to promote the values of "diversity, inclusiveness and dignity," central components in CS's business. The firm has also been ranked as one of the top 100 companies for working mothers.

Please describe any diversity hiring efforts in regards to gays and lesbians.

The firm received a 100 percent rating on the Human Rights Campaign Corporate Equality Index for gay, lesbian, bisexual and transgender employees

Visit the Vault Finance Career Channel at **www.vault.com/finance** — with
insider firm profiles, message boards, the Vault Finance Job Board and more.

VAULT CAREER LIBRARY   **125**

Deutsche Bank Private Wealth Management

Deutsche Bank AG Taunusanlage 12 60325 Frankfurt am Main Phone: +49 69 910-00 Fax: +49 69 910-34 225 E-mail: eutsche.bank@db.com www.db.com **EMPLOYMENT CONTACT** www.db.com/careers	**Chairman:** Clemens Börsig **CEO:** Josef Ackermann **Firm Type:** Public Company **2005 Total Firm Revenue (Worldwide):** Euro 25.640 billion **2005 Total Firm Net Income (Worldwide):** Euro 3.529 billion **No. of Employees (Private Wealth):** 3,300 (1,000 in the U.S.) **No. of Employees (Firmwide):** 63,427 **No. of Office Locations (Worldwide):** 1,559

Hiring Process

Recruiting

Deutsche Bank recruits on campus for analyst positions at more than 40 universities in the U.S., less than half of which are Ivy League. These universities are chosen based on factors, such as academic reputation, our historic hiring relationship with the school, specific attractive degree disciplines (business, engineering, etc.), numbers of students meeting our criteria and engagement of internal DB alumni champions.

In addition to our target list—where we are fully active on campus—we also accept applications from any other schools via our online application system. We have an "Open Day" interview process in place to target these students. Annually, some 20 percent of our U.S. hires are sourced from outside our target school list.

Visit Vault at **www.vault.com** for insider company profiles, expert advice, career message boards, expert resume reviews, the Vault Job Board and more.

VAULT CAREER LIBRARY 127

For undergrads, we annually recruit at Ivy League schools (such as Harvard, Princeton and Wharton), public state schools (such as the University of Michigan), private schools and other institutions.

For grad students, we annually recruit at MBA programs (such as Columbia, Chicago and MIT) and other graduate schools in programs other than MBA (such as Rutgers and Morehouse).

Where else does your firm recruit for employees?

Our recruiting tools are as varied as the candidates we are looking for. Whether it is job postings in relevant publications, banners on career web sites or participating at fairs, Deutsche Bank tries to attract suitable candidates through all kinds of channels.

Hiring

What are the position titles for new hires coming out of undergrad? Out of grad school?

Undergraduates usually enter graduate programs as analysts, and MBAs enter the graduate programs as associates.

Please describe the hiring process at your firm.

Hiring processes vary by location as do campus events. All applications, however, are submitted via our online application tool. Eligible applications are then forwarded to the business representatives and, if selected, a first interview is scheduled. The number of interview rounds differs by country and division. Candidates must be prepared to tell us why they are right for Deutsche Bank and why Deutsche Bank is right for them. They need to be serious about an investment banking career and be familiar with financial concepts.

What are some of the requirements for jobs?

Successful candidates are client and relationship focused, have a healthy intellectual curiosity, excellent analytical skills and the ability to deliver. We accept applications from all disciplines with a bachelor degree for full time positions or pending degrees for internships. In general we expect solid academic records, although we aim at looking at the whole individual instead of grades only.

Other requirements include excellent communication and teamwork skills, creative problem solving abilities, a desire to achieve results, strong analytical aptitude. Combined with an affinity for capital markets and securities, candidates should demonstrate personal integrity and a commitment to exceed the highest professional standards. Foreign language proficiency is a plus, and candidates usually require a relevant work permit.

Please describe your summer internships.

We offer a wide range of internships at different locations worldwide. As we are offering internships at all kinds of locations, they often differ from one place to the other. Regarding our positions in private wealth management, internships can be completed in the U.S., U.K., China and Singapore, where they last from nine to 10 weeks and in Germany lasting up to six months. Interns are given the opportunity to work alongside experienced professionals, complete real time projects, work on live deals and be paid competitively. In addition, Deutsche Bank offers networking events with peers and representatives, and at some locations also classroom training. Internships have in the past proven to be invaluable to recruiting valuable talents. Currently we aim at offering about 60 percent of our successful interns a permanent position after their placement. Salaries are highly competitive.

Inside the Firm: Culture and Training

Please describe the corporate culture at your firm.

At Deutsche Bank our corporate culture is intensely shaped by the values we adhere to, which mainly consist of the following:

Performance — We are committed to a result-oriented culture.

Trust — We behave reliably, fairly and honestly.

Teamwork — We benefit from the diversity of our business and our people by working together to achieve success.

Innovation — We are constantly challenging conventional wisdom and developing new solutions to meet customer requirements.

Client Focus — We place customers at the centre of our activities and they drive all that we do.

These values stem into the "One Bank" concept, which highlights our meritocracy based "One Team" philosophy.

Please describe any mentoring programs at your firm.

Mentoring is a valuable tool for career development, gaining organizational knowledge and building an internal network. Deutsche Bank currently employs

Visit the Vault Finance Career Channel at **www.vault.com/finance** — with
insider firm profiles, message boards, the Vault Finance Job Board and more.

VAULT CAREER LIBRARY   **129**

various formal mentoring programs which are to be further expanded as part of our global diversity strategy.

Please describe any formal training programs for employees.

The induction training program starts with global orientation where it is our aim to provide analysts with an introduction to the structure, history, strategic direction and culture of Deutsche Bank. This is followed by a teambuilding event with graduates from all divisions. Working with private wealth management graduates from all over the world, analysts will gain a thorough understanding of the technical skills required as well as the more interpersonal aspects. The whole training program is based in London and lasts approximately six weeks. Extensive further training is continuously being offered during the placement period and afterwards.

Compensation

Please describe compensation and other monetary benefits at your firm.

Salaries are highly competitive.

Hours

On average, how many hours do professionals work in the office per week?

Varies but certainly over 40.

Diversity

At Deutsche Bank, we are committed to recruiting, retaining and developing diverse talent. We think of diversity in its broadest sense, embracing all of those differences that make up the exciting challenging world in which we live. These include age, culture, ethnicity, gender, nationality, personality type, physical ability, religion, sexual orientation and work style.

A homogeneous workforce does not generate new ways of thinking. Diverse perspectives foster innovation and creativity. They enable us to build teams with a unique range of capabilities that can win the trust of our most demanding clients. They enhance our ability to respond to global business issues and provide innovative, superior solutions. That's why, for us, diversity is a business imperative, improving performance for clients, employees and shareholders alike.

Recognizing diversity is important, but not enough on its own. That is why we have invested in diversity, embedding it into the fabric of our organization. Deutsche Bank leverages its diversity and fosters a work environment that attracts, develops and retains a diverse pool of talent.

Visit the Vault Finance Career Channel at **www.vault.com/finance** — with
insider firm profiles, message boards, the Vault Finance Job Board and more.

VAULT CAREER LIBRARY   131

Fifth Third Asset Management

Fifth Third Bancorp Fifth Third Center Cincinnati, OH 45263 Phone: (513) 534-5300 Fax: (513) 579-6246 www.53.com **EMPLOYMENT CONTACT** cvg53.recruitmax.com	**Chairman & CEO:** George A Schaefer Jr. **Firm Type:** Public Company **2005 Private Wealth Management Revenue (Worldwide):** $234.3 million **2005 Total Firm Revenue (Worldwide):** $5.5 billion **2005 Total Firm Net Income (Worldwide):** $1.54 billion **No. of Employees (Firmwide):** 21,681 **No. of Office Locations (Worldwide):** 19 affiliates with 1,119 banking centers

Hiring Process

Recruiting

The firm recruits on college campuses, primarily in the Midwest. Candidates can also create a profile with a resume and cover letter for the firm's searchable online database. The profile can be saved and used to apply directly to jobs posted on the web site.

What are some of the requirements for jobs?

The investment advisors division is in search of candidates with a well-rounded background that includes academic achievement, extracurricular involvement and the drive to be the best. Candidates should also have earned a bachelor's degree in business administration, finance, economics or accounting, with a cumulative GPA of 3.0 or higher. Preference will be given to candidates with sales experience and/or experience in an investment environment.

Inside the Firm: Culture and Training

Please describe any scholarship programs at your firm.

The firm offers a Forgiveness Loan Program to help employees finance tuition costs. Employees who remain with the firm for one year after completing the course do not have to repay the loan. Full-time employees are eligible to receive tuition reimbursement of $5,000 per year, and part-time employees are eligible to receive $1,000.

Please describe any ongoing or other training programs for employees.

Our senior management, as well as all of our managers, participates in diversity training to foster the recognition of differences as virtues.

Compensation

Please describe compensation and other monetary benefits at your firm.

The firm offers a profit sharing plan paid out annually based on bank performance, which vests after five years of employment. Employees can also participate in a matched 401(k) plan and an employee common stock purchase plan, with 15 percent matched by the firm. In addition, the bank offers mortgage loan discounts and several free banking services.

Diversity

Please describe any diversity hiring efforts in regards to minorities.

Supervisors, department heads and all employees share responsibility for the affirmative action program, which is monitored and evaluated continuously to ensure that the equal employment opportunity policy is successful.

Friedman Billings Ramsey
Investment Management

1001 Nineteenth Street North Arlington, VA 22209 Phone: (703) 312-9500 Fax: (703) 312-9501 www.fbr.com **EMPLOYMENT CONTACT** www.fbr.com/company/work	**Chairman & CEO:** Eric F. Billings **Firm Type:** Public Company **2005 Total Firm Revenue (Worldwide):** $1.0 billion **2005 Total Firm Net Income (Worldwide):** ($170.9) million **No. of Employees (Firmwide):** 850 **No. of Office Locations (Worldwide):** 12

Hiring Process

Hiring

What are some of the requirements for jobs (GPA, degree, personality, skills, etc.)?

For internships, a major in finance, business administration, accounting, computer science or human resources is preferred.

Please describe your summer internships.

The firm believes "a strong internship program is the best way to recruit future FBR leaders."

Compensation

Please describe compensation and other monetary benefits at your firm.

The firm offers a 401(k), an employee stock purchase plan, health care spending and dependent care spending accounts (pre-tax deduction options), public transportation and parking reimbursement accounts (pre-tax deductions), paid time off, an employee referral program and tuition reimbursement.

Please describe other perks.

The firm has an on-site fitness facility, and offers daily breakfast and lunch, emergency back up child care, an employee assistance program, learning and development, and medical, dental, disability, travel accident and life insurance.

Great minds don't always think alike.

Here we embrace those with a different point of view. Because the challenges we face come in many different forms, it takes many different kinds of people to meet them. Are you one of them?

Please visit **gs.com/careers** to complete an online application.

Goldman Sachs Private Wealth Management

85 Broad Street New York, NY 10004 Phone: (212) 902-1000 Fax: (212) 902-3000 www.gs.com **EMPLOYMENT CONTACT** gs.com/careers	**Chairman & CEO:** Lloyd C. Blankfein **Firm Type:** Public Company **2005 Total Firm Revenue (Worldwide):** $24.79 billion (FYE 11/2005) **2005 Total Firm Net Income (Worldwide):** $5.63 billion **No. of Employees (Firmwide):** 22,425 **No. of Office Locations (Firmwide):** 45

Hiring Process

Recruiting

For undergrads, the firm annually recruits at top colleges and universities in the U.S. and abroad. For graduate school students, the firm annually recruits at top MBA programs and JD programs.

Where else does your firm recruit for employees?

Resumes can be submitted at gs.com/careers, and the firm also recruits at school career centers and through outside agencies and job fairs.

Hiring

For PWM, what are the position titles for new hires coming out of undergrad? Out of grad school?

Undergrad: financial analyst. Graduate school: associate.

Visit Vault at **www.vault.com** for insider company profiles, expert advice, career message boards, expert resume reviews, the Vault Job Board and more.

VAULT CAREER LIBRARY   137

Please describe the hiring process at your firm.

For campus applicants, events on campus can vary by school, but typically include information sessions, targeted events and first-round interviews. Candidates are interviewed through several rounds and will meet investment professionals across our business during this process. For more information about our hiring process, please visit gs.com/careers.

What are some of the requirements for jobs?

Overall, we look to recruit talent who can build relationships and assist our clients with their wealth preservation and growth. Our Private Wealth Management (PWM) teams work one-on-one with clients to deliver customized strategies drawn from our deep investment experience, diverse investment vehicles and global reach. As client needs evolve, this close relationship allows the team to offer complementary products and services as well as new opportunities. Our ability to offer clients superior service is predicated on recruiting exceptional talent and having one of the most rigorous training programs in our industry.

Undergraduate requirements:

• College or university degree

• Record of academic excellence

• Proven leadership ability

• Demonstrated interest in and knowledge of finance, economics and global capital markets

• Strong organizational skills

• Excellent interpersonal skills and a desire to work in a team-oriented environment

• Creative approach to problem solving

• Strong analytical and communication skills

• Resourceful, energetic, detail oriented

• Ability to multitask in a fast-paced environment

• Commitment to excellence

• High integrity

MBA requirements:

• Advanced degree

• Two to five years of work experience

- Record of academic excellence

- Proven leadership ability

- Motivated by having compensation closely aligned with performance and results

- Demonstrated interest in and knowledge of finance, economics and global capital markets

- Excellent interpersonal skills and a desire to work in a team-oriented environment; connects well with people; likeable, empathetic, sense of humor; able to build a strong network of relationships

- Strong client focus and relationship management skills

- Creative approach to problem solving with good business acumen

- Strong analytical and communication skills

- Resourcefulness, energy, attention to detail and the ability to multitask in a fast-paced environment

- Commitment to excellence and high integrity

Please describe your summer internships.

- We have a 10-week summer internship for both summer analysts and summer associates. Our summer interns receive competitive salaries and are paid bi-monthly.

- Both summer analysts and associates for Private Wealth Management (PWM) receive an in-depth overview of the Investment Management Division, its businesses and its clients. Summer interns also are provided many opportunities to build a network of relationships throughout the firm.

Summer Analyst Program

- PWM summer analysts receive formal training pertaining to the Private Wealth Management business, including the sales cycle and our products as well as the desktop tools they will use during their internship.

- As a summer intern, analysts take on various responsibilities including the following:

  - Working closely with investment professionals to stay on top of client needs
  - Keeping abreast of the latest event in the markets
  - Relaying Goldman Sachs research to investment professionals

Visit the Vault Finance Career Channel at **www.vault.com/finance** — with insider firm profiles, message boards, the Vault Finance Job Board and more.

V/\ULT CAREER LIBRARY   **139**

- Developing and preparing marketing presentations that address equity fixed income and alternative investments, asset allocation and external manager selection
- Analyzing client equity and fixed income portfolios
- Assisting on projects related to new business development, strategic planning, asset allocation, product development and other marketing infrastructure issues
- Working in conjunction with various product groups within the Investment Management Division to respond to client needs
- Providing client service and team support

Summer Associate Program

- PWM summer associates can expect a structured learning experience that will entail various professional and technical training programs as well as assisting current investment professionals with their day-to-day work. The curriculum has been developed to provide an in-depth view of the role of an investment professional and the sales cycle. Individual and team-based assignments, presentations and interactive discussions have been designed to build on each other to help summer associates better understand the breadth of investment strategies and services that Goldman Sachs offers, how we utilize those strategies and services, and the investment process and sales cycle. As a result, summer associates are introduced to professionals throughout our asset management and products and services areas over the course of the summer.

- The presentations and discussions will provide summer associates with the tools and knowledge they will need, while assigned projects will provide them with the opportunity to apply the concepts learned in simulated exercises. Summer associates will also observe and learn from a diverse group of investment professionals how to respond to client needs using simulated case studies. In addition, summer associates learn the typical day of an investment professional by job-shadowing and assisting our current investment professionals throughout their internship.

- The 10-week internship is also complemented by a regional rotation. All summer associates hired by offices other than New York will spend seven weeks in New York and three weeks in their regional hiring office. Summer associates hired by New York PWM will also have the opportunity to rotate in an office other than New York for a period of one week to gain a better understanding of specific regional characteristics and dynamics.

Inside the Firm: Culture and Training (Firmwide)

Please describe the corporate culture at your firm.

The Goldman Sachs culture is what sets our company apart from other firms and helps to make us a magnet for talent. Our commitment to clients, teamwork, integrity, professional excellence and entrepreneurial spirit has its beginnings in 1869 with Marcus Goldman. This spirit is embodied today in our core values of client focus, integrity, meritocracy, excellence, entrepreneurial spirit and teamwork. At the core of our business is our commitment to our clients, embodied in our 14 business principles, a consistent measure for evaluating recruits and employees.

To maintain our competitive edge and meet the high expectations of our clients, our culture continues to evolve. Goldman Sachs has made a commitment to creating an environment that values diversity and promotes inclusion. Additionally, the people of Goldman Sachs take very seriously their responsibility to the communities where they live and work. Besides being responsive to community needs, Goldman Sachs has a longstanding tradition of leadership in philanthropy through various organizations worldwide.

Please describe any mentoring programs at your firm.

PWM summer interns are assigned mentors, who are Goldman Sachs employees within the division, to help guide them through their summer at the firm. In addition, the firm encourages mentoring and provides access to mentors for all new employees, including our new full-time analysts and associates.

Please describe any scholarship programs at your firm.

Goldman Sachs sponsors scholarship programs to promote diversity within the financial services industry. These include the Scholarship for Excellence (for undergraduates) and the MBA Fellowship (for MBAs). Aside from the scholarships, we offer special programming and career camps for diverse candidates. For more information, please visit our Careers site.

Please describe any formal training programs for employees.

Through Goldman Sachs University (GSU), we offer comprehensive orientation training programs for both new and experienced hires to ensure they are equipped with the knowledge and skills necessary to succeed. This includes acculturation into the firm and the division, technical and product training, selling and other professional skills and compliance.

Visit the Vault Finance Career Channel at **www.vault.com/finance** — with insider firm profiles, message boards, the Vault Finance Job Board and more.

VAULT CAREER LIBRARY   **141**

Please describe any ongoing or other training programs for employees.

Goldman Sachs has a strong commitment to continuing education. Our employees can take advantage of financial markets training ranging from fundamentals to advanced applications, including Goldman Sachs businesses and products offered through Goldman Sachs University. GSU also has a broad offering of various professional skills and leadership training. Our courses leverage the expertise of both internal experts and external consultants.

Compensation

Please describe compensation and other monetary benefits at your firm.

We have competitive compensation packages.

Please describe other perks.

Please visit our careers site for more information about our Wellness Exchange, which provides numerous resources to help employees balance their work and personal lives: www.gs.com/careers/about_goldman_sachs/wellness_exchange

Hours

On average, how many hours do professionals work in the office per week?

It can vary between 50 to 60 and 60 to 70 hours per week.

How often do they work on weekends?

Rarely.

Please comment on workload/hours.

The benefit to PWM is that the hours and workload are predictable. Professionals know when to expect longer days and can plan accordingly.

Diversity (Firmwide)

Diversity recruiting programs

Goldman Sachs has initiated and currently manages a number of programs designed to increase awareness of the firm and our industry within diverse communities.

These programs allow us to offer academic scholarships, educational opportunities, summer internships and full-time positions to many outstanding students. Not all of these students have a finance or business background; we actively seek candidates from a broad array of academic disciplines and concentrations such as liberal arts, applied math, sciences and engineering, in order to reach a wide spectrum of strong candidates.

GS Scholars

In 1998, Goldman Sachs launched the GS Scholars Program to work with promising young students from historically underrepresented groups, introducing them to the world of business and finance. Many of these students have gone on to hold summer internships and full-time positions with the firm. Students affiliated with select nonprofit partners are eligible to apply for the Goldman Sachs Scholars Program at the end of their senior year of high school. Students who are selected as Goldman Sachs Scholars will participate in the program through their sophomore year in college. Goldman Sachs Scholars learn about the business world and the financial services industry through a series of four seminars conducted over two years (summers and winters of their freshman and sophomore years) in New York. This includes initial visits focusing on building professional skills and networking, seminars explaining the various lines of business in financial services, and a four-day camp focusing on leadership skills and careers in business. Each Scholar is also matched up with a "Big Buddy," a Goldman Sachs professional who will serve as their mentor.

Nonprofit organizations we partner with: A Better Chance , 4XL™, Jackie Robinson Foundation, I-Lead Bank Street, LEAD Program in Business, New Jersey Seeds, Posse Foundation, Prep for Prep, SEO Scholars and the Teak Foundation.

Goldman Sachs Scholarship for Excellence

Established in 1994, the Goldman Sachs Scholarship for Excellence (SFE) program was initially created to increase the level of interest in and awareness of careers in the industry among students at historically black colleges and universities. Today, the scholarship has expanded to target black, Hispanic and Native American undergraduate students at all of the firm's target undergraduate schools.

Recipients of the scholarship completing their sophomore year of college receive a $5,000 award toward tuition and academic expenses for one year. Students invited to return for a second summer internship are eligible to receive an additional award

Visit the Vault Finance Career Channel at **www.vault.com/finance** — with insider firm profiles, message boards, the Vault Finance Job Board and more.

VAULT CAREER LIBRARY   **143**

of $7,500. Recipients completing their junior year receive a scholarship award of $7,500. All scholarship recipients also receive an offer for a paid Goldman Sachs summer internship.

Goldman Sachs MBA Fellowship Program

Initiated in 1997, Goldman Sachs MBA Fellowship Program is designed to increase the level of interest in and awareness of careers in the industry among black and Hispanic business school students. Through the program, Goldman Sachs offers 10 fellowships to students from up to 10 target graduate business schools annually. The Goldman Sachs MBA Fellowship is offered at the following schools: Columbia Business School, Duke University-The Fuqua School of Business, Harvard Business School, Massachusetts Institute of Technology-Sloan School of Management, Northwestern University-Kellogg School of Management, Stanford Graduate School of Business, University of California at Los Angeles-Anderson School of Management, University of Chicago-Graduate School of Business, University of Michigan-Ross School of Business and University of Pennsylvania-The Wharton School.

Goldman Sachs MBA Fellows will receive full tuition for the first year of business school and a summer associate position between the first and second year of school. Second-year tuition will be awarded contingent upon receipt and acceptance of a full-time offer. Potential candidates for the program are referred to the firm with the help of the admissions and financial aid offices. Fellows are assigned mentors within the division in which they are placed for their summer associate work experience. Fellows act as ambassadors on campus to educate others in their communities about Goldman Sachs and the financial services industry. They are also instrumental in sharing recruiting best practices at their respective schools.

Gay and Lesbian Recruiting Events and Conferences

In 1999, Goldman Sachs became one of the first investment banks to offer recruiting events for the gay and lesbian student clubs at our target business schools. Each year we offer a series of dinners for MBA student clubs in several different cities in conjunction with our Gay and Lesbian Network (GALN). The firm is also a sponsor of "Reaching Out," the annual MBA business conference for gay and lesbian students from business schools nationwide. During the summer, the GALN offers a Pride month reception for summer associates and students from local business schools. In

October 2004, the firm was one of the charter sponsors of the first gay and lesbian conference for undergraduate students held at Cornell University.

GS Camp—for MBAs & Undergrads

Since 1999, Goldman has been offering the MBA camp for black, Hispanic and Native American students without prior financial services experience to explore the investment banking industry before entering business school. In 2005, Goldman launched a similarly modeled undergraduate version, "GS Undergraduate Camp." The two-and-a-half day programs include case studies, divisional presentations, career workshops and social events. Through these events, Goldman Sachs meets potential candidates for summer intern positions months in advance (for MBAs) and years in advance (for undergrads) of the formal interview process.

Annual Undergraduate Women's Summit

Held for the first time in February 2005, the Undergraduate Women's Summit attracts women from the best liberal arts colleges underserved by Goldman Sachs and premiere women's colleges to attend a daylong educational and networking event. Select attendees are interviewed and considered for summer analyst positions.

Annual MBA Women's Summit

Goldman Sachs hosts a daylong educational and networking event for over 100 first year women MBA students. Designed to encourage women to apply for summer associate positions, the MBA Women's Summit addresses the issues of diversity, work/life and long-term career opportunities.

Annual Undergraduate Diversity Summit

Since January 2006, the Undergraduate Diversity Summit attracts students affiliated with our nonprofit partners, including the National Society of Black Engineers (NSBE), Management Leadership for Tomorrow (MLT) and LEAD. Attendees participate in the daylong event that features divisional overviews, interviewing and networking sessions.

School Sponsored Diversity Conferences

The firm financially supports and participates in various conferences sponsored by minority and women organizations at our target graduate business schools. We have

Visit the Vault Finance Career Channel at **www.vault.com/finance** — with insider firm profiles, message boards, the Vault Finance Job Board and more.

VAULT CAREER LIBRARY   145

also participated in major diversity conferences at Harvard Business School, University of Michigan Business School, Fuqua (Duke), Stern (NYU) and Columbia Business School.

Nonprofit Organizations and Conferences

The firm has been a long standing supporter of many career and professional development organizations, such as NSHMBA, NBMBAA, NAWMBA, SHPE, NSBE, ALPFA, NABA and HACE. Every year, Goldman sponsors and attends national conferences hosted by these organizations in an effort to attract and source diverse talent for the firm. The firm has also sponsored numerous initiatives and workshops that are offered to professional and student members of these organizations.

Additional Information

Goldman Sachs is a leading global investment banking, securities and investment management firm that provides a wide range of services worldwide to a substantial and diversified client base that includes corporations, financial institutions, governments and high-net-worth individuals. Founded in 1869, it is one of the oldest and largest investment banking firms. The firm is headquartered in New York, and maintains offices in London, Frankfurt, Tokyo, Hong Kong and other major financial centers around the world.

Goldman Sachs Private Wealth Management is committed to being the chief investment officer to the wealthiest and most influential families in the area and in the world. To play that role, we combine discipline, innovation and focus in seeking to provide our clients with: excellent investment performance and client service; industry-leading guidance and insights into the global economy and its markets; and exclusive investment products and advisory services.

Investing in today's environment is, by necessity, a dynamic process. The financial markets are highly interdependent and successful investment portfolios require a global perspective and individualized strategy. Goldman Sachs has developed a range of investment services and products that are among the most comprehensive in the industry, including:

- Complete Asset Allocation and Portfolio Strategy
- Full Range of Financial Counseling Services
- Evaluation of Estate Planning and Trust Services from the GS Trust Company

- Coordination with Accountants and Attorneys
- Sophisticated Cash Management Techniques
- Pre-IPO Wealth Planning and Post-IPO Diversification Strategies
- Industry Leadership in Restricted Equities Sales
- Employee Stock Option Strategies
- Private Banking Services

Goldman Sachs provides clients with a level of investment research, trading execution and personalized wealth services that most firms afford only their institutional investors. We actively participate in most major world markets. This allows us to remain on the cutting edge of investment techniques and provides us with a complete picture of the global investment environment. This translates into thoughtful and ultimately cost effective investment advice, and an exceptional level of service. For more information about career opportunities please visit gs.com/careers.

Visit the Vault Finance Career Channel at **www.vault.com/finance** — with
insider firm profiles, message boards, the Vault Finance Job Board and more.

VAULT CAREER LIBRARY   **147**

HSBC Private Bank

World Headquarters 8 Canada Square London E14 5HQ United Kingdom Phone: +44 020 7991 8888 Fax: +44 020 7992 4880 HSBC Bank USA 452 Fifth Avenue New York, NY 10018 Phone: (212) 525-5000 www.us.hsbc.com **EMPLOYMENT CONTACT** www.hsbcprivatebank.com/hsbc/rhp/careers	**Firm Chairman:** Stephen K. Green **Firm CEO:** Michael Geoghegan **Firm President, CEO & Director, HSBC USA:** Sandy Derickson **Firm Type:** Public Company **2005 Private Wealth Management Pretax Profit (North America):** $104 million **2005 Private Wealth Management Pretax Profit (Worldwide):** $912 million **2005 Total Firm Revenue (Worldwide):** $93.4 billion **2005 Total Firm Net Income (Worldwide):** $15.4 billion **No. of Employees (Private Wealth):** 5,500 **No. of Employees (Firmwide):** 279,393 **No. of Office Locations (Worldwide):** 9,800+

Hiring Process

Hiring

Please describe the hiring process at your firm.

There are four stages to the graduate recruitment process. The first step is the online application form, and the second stage is online testing. If you are selected to

Visit Vault at **www.vault.com** for insider company profiles, expert advice,
career message boards, expert resume reviews, the Vault Job Board and more.

VAULT CAREER LIBRARY   149

continue the process, a first interview will take place over the phone or in person. The last step is testing at assessment center. Our assessment centers are two-way events. They're not just designed to help us decide if you're right for us, they help you decide if we're right for you. You'll have plenty of opportunities to find out more about what it's like to work for HSBC, and the kind of roles you could be doing.

The assessment center revolves around a variety of one-to-one and group-based activities that give you the chance to display the key capabilities we look for in our graduates. We'll give you a clear brief at the beginning of each exercise and there are no tricks or hidden agendas. We won't try to trip you up—we genuinely want to give you the best chance to show us what you're capable of.

On the private bank careers page of the firm's web site, there is more information on what to expect and how to prepare for the interview and assessment center.

What are some of the requirements for jobs?

The firm is looking for creative thinkers—people who don't always assume the obvious or accept conventional wisdom; good bankers learn to expect the unexpected. The other essential requirements are: strong business English and fluency in at least two other languages; global mobility for the duration of the program, combined with cultural sensitivity and awareness; high levels of numeracy and commercial judgment; intellectual agility and a willingness to challenge the status quo; and a strong client focus.

Please describe your summer internships.

HSBC Private Bank offers a structured 10-week summer internship program. First of all, a comprehensive induction gives an introduction to how we operate. Private wealth management summer analysts spend nine weeks fully aligned to one of the business teams, working on a variety of projects and making a real contribution.

On top of this there'll be further formal training plus a busy calendar of business briefings, workshops and social events. What's more, you'll have the chance to get to know people across the business and to build a network of other interns, graduate trainees and senior business managers—a network you'll find invaluable should you join the bank long term.

The firm sets the same standards and selection criteria for interns as it does for graduates. Therefore, there are four stages to the internship recruitment process: online application form, online tests, first interview and a day at the assessment center.

Inside the Firm: Culture and Training

Please describe any formal training programs for employees.

HSBC Private Bank's graduate program introduces new hires to all aspects of the firm's global business—including frontline client relationship management, operational and support functions, and our product development environment.

After the initial nine-week training period (five at the U.K.-based Management Training College at Bricket Wood in Hertfordshire and four in London) and regulatory exams, you'll begin the first of three six-month rotations within the private bank. We'll structure your rotations to give you exposure to technical products and relationship management, and show you how support functions contribute to the success of the business. We'll also support you in studying for the chartered financial analyst (CFA) qualification. To support your career development, you will be appointed an "underwriter" who will oversee your progress. You'll also be appointed a mentor, who by the nature of the role, will not be directly responsible for your rotations or direct career development but will provide guidance, support and encouragement throughout the program. To help you gain a real overview of the business, your rotations will be in a number of locations. Possible rotations include Singapore, Geneva, London or New York.

Please describe any ongoing or other training programs for employees.

No matter where employees begin their careers at HSBC, the firm offers professional development, mentoring and training opportunities that can help them develop their talents throughout their careers. Employees can take advantage of hundreds of business-specific and professional development training resources (classroom instruction, self-study programs, peer training and web-based training) to help develop and enhance their skills. Through several management training programs in our business units, we offer rotational job assignments, mentoring, networking and formal training to high-potential employees to help them become leaders. Our business and operating units have implemented special mentoring programs that pair high-potential individuals with business-savvy senior managers to provide advice, collaborate on career development and increase visibility with the HSBC leadership team.

Employees receive regular performance evaluation. Managers work with their employees to set performance goals and expectations and evaluate progress toward the employee's professional development goals. At our larger locations, employees can learn more on their own by visiting our corporate libraries stocked with books, tapes, periodicals and, in some cases, Internet-ready personal computers.

Visit the Vault Finance Career Channel at **www.vault.com/finance** — with insider firm profiles, message boards, the Vault Finance Job Board and more.

V/\ULT CAREER LIBRARY   **151**

Compensation

Please describe compensation and other monetary benefits at your firm.

In addition to salary, employees of the private bank receive a performance related bonus. The firm offers a pension plan for employees.

Please describe other perks.

Employees receive preferential rates on a range of HSBC products. In addition, a season ticket loan, a sports and social scheme and various corporate discounts are among other benefits.

Diversity

Please describe any diversity hiring efforts in regards to women.

HSBC has several employee networks throughout the organization that support diversity efforts. The Women's Forum assists with recruiting and promoting professional development through networking and mentoring programs.

Please describe any diversity hiring efforts in regards to minorities.

Our HSBC-North America diversity initiatives are led by a cross-functional diversity council, which promotes understanding of business issues within the context of diversity through leadership and education. The 26-member council helps our organization identify best practices in diversity recruitment, talent development, supplier/partner community building and overall strategy, and provides employees a voice within the organization.

HSBC-North America maintains a strong commitment to attracting and engaging diverse talent, and we partner with premier professional associations and civic organizations that help us identify and recruit the leaders of tomorrow. The firm has partnerships with INROADS, the National Association of Asian American Professionals, National Black MBA Association, National Society of Hispanic MBAs, NAACP, National Urban League, United Negro College Fund, Hispanic Alliance for College Education and the Urban Financial Services Coalition.

Please describe any diversity hiring efforts in regards to gays and lesbians.

The firm has a GLBT group which assists with recruiting and promoting professional development of diverse employees through industry networking and mentoring programs.

Additional Information

HSBC Private Bank is the marketing name for the private banking business conducted by the principal private banking subsidiaries of the HSBC Group worldwide. HSBC Private Bank, together with HSBC Guyerzeller and the private banking and trustee activities of HSBC Trinkaus & Burkhardt, provides private banking and trustee services to high-net-worth individuals and their families through 82 locations in the Americas, the Asia-Pacific region, Europe and the Middle East. As of June 30, 2006, profits before tax were $600 million for the half year and combined client assets under management were $371 billion. We employ over 5,500 staff worldwide. Drawing on the strength of the HSBC Group and the best products from the marketplace, we work with our clients to develop innovative solutions to manage, preserve and develop wealth for now and for future generations.

The private banking division offers investment planning, wealth planning, specialist advisory services, and financial and banking services. Private banking is one of HSBC's five strategic customer groups, the others being personal financial services, consumer finance, commercial banking, and corporate, investment banking and markets.

Jefferies Private Client Services

520 Madison Avenue
12th floor
New York, NY 10022
Phone: (212) 284-2300
Fax: (212) 284-2111
www.jefferies.com

EMPLOYMENT
CONTACT

Michele Vespi
Phone: (212) 284-2300
Fax: (212) 284-2111
E-mail: info@jefferies.com

Career web site address:
See careers at
www.jefferies.com

Firm Chairman & CEO: Richard B. Handler
Firm Type: Public Company
2005 Total Firm Revenue (Worldwide): $1.5 billion
2005 Total Firm Net Income (Worldwide): $157.4 million
No. of Employees (Firmwide): 2,045
No. of Office Locations (Worldwide): 25+

Hiring Process

Recruiting

The firm's private client services group does not recruit on campus. Candidates can search for jobs and submit a resume on the career page of the firm's web site.

Additional Information

Jefferies private client services group provides financial services to corporate clients and their senior executives, private equity firms, middle market institutions and high-net-worth individuals. Products and services include equity trading, fixed income, mutual funds, structured notes and separately managed accounts through outside money managers, including funds of hedge funds. Our financial professionals create customized strategies to fulfill our clients' objectives and distinguish themselves by their objectivity and customer focus.

As a natural extension of Jefferies' full-service platform, our professionals work closely with our powerful institutional equity sales and trading platform, and offer access to our award-winning equity research.

JPMorgan Private Bank

270 Park Ave.
New York, NY 10017
Phone: (212) 270-6000
Fax: (212)270-1648
www.jpmorganchase.com

**EMPLOYMENT
CONTACT**

careers.jpmorganchase.com

Firm President & CEO: James A. Dimon
Firm Type: Public Company
**2005 Private Bank Revenue
(Worldwide):** $1.68 billion
**2005 Total Firm Revenue
(Worldwide):** $54.72 billion
**2005 Total Firm Net Income
(Worldwide):** $11.84 billion
No. of Employees (Private Bank):
67
No. of Employees (Firmwide):
168,847
**No. of Office Locations
(Worldwide):** Operations in more
than 50 countries

Hiring Process

Recruiting

The Private Bank actively recruits from at both undergraduate and graduate schools across the U.S.

Core schools for the undergraduate analyst program are: NYU, University of Virginia, Boston College, Cornell, Yale, Georgetown, University of Texas, Michigan, William & Mary, Stanford, Berkley, Columbia, Duke, Babson, University of Pennsylvania and Fordham.

Core schools for the graduate associate program are: NYU, Columbia, Harvard, University of Virginia, Dartmouth, University of Texas, University of Chicago, Northwestern, Duke, Wharton, Michigan and University of North Carolina.

Where else does your firm recruit for employees (job postings, web sites, other firms, etc.)?

On the firm's web site, candidates can search for jobs that match skills and interests. To apply for a position, follow the application directions to submit a resume. Candidates have the option to build a profile so that opportunities matching specific search criteria can be automatically e-mailed to you.

Hiring

What are the position titles for new hires coming out of undergrad? Out of grad school?

Analyst (Undergraduate)

The three-year analyst program provides exposure to multiple business areas within the Private Bank. Analysts are placed in a banking, investment or product team analyst role. As you progress in your analyst role, you will assume significant responsibility by working directly with clients while interacting frequently with senior management.

As a Private Banking analyst, you will support a banker, a product specialist or a global investment specialist. Depending on your role, you will help to acquire new clients and service existing clients, use sophisticated, proprietary asset allocation, wealth projection and concentrated stock and option decision tools, and conduct market and product research. You will make a valuable contribution to a team providing integrated delivery of financial solutions.

Private Banking analysts support teams in various locations throughout the U.S., including New York, Chicago, Philadelphia, Washington, D.C., Atlanta, Palm Beach, Dallas, Houston, Denver, San Francisco and Los Angeles.

Associate (Graduate)

Associates are primarily hired to serve as a banker, global investment specialist or product specialist. The banker and global investment specialist roles both require a complete and deep understanding of a client's situation, ranging from their wealth objectives to their risk tolerance to what they want their legacy to be. The product specialist role requires the ability to create innovative and cutting-edge investment solutions to ensure a client's investment needs are met across major asset classes.

As a banker, you focus on new business and on existing clients' overall relationship with the Private Bank to ensure that client needs are met across many spectrums such as banking, lending, and trust and estate planning.

As a global investment specialist, you provide clients with access to global research, asset allocation advice, products and trade execution. You interact with clients who are managing their own portfolios. You also help clients execute strategies for managing their options, low-basis stock and restricted stock. You play a critical role in business development efforts.

As a product specialist, you provide external and internal clients with the expertise you develop in one of many complex financial products, such as equity derivatives or alternative assets. You may also work with the individuals who deliver our strategic viewpoints, or those who construct optimal portfolios for our clients.

Positions are generally available in New York and other major U.S. cities (covering clients in the Americas), as well as in Asia.

What are some of the requirements for jobs?

Analyst (Undergraduate)

Candidates should have a strong interest in investments as evidenced through prior experience, and strong analytical skills for both qualitative and quantitative analysis of complex financial situations. Excellent communication and interpersonal skills are required, and candidates should have the initiative, energy and confidence to complete projects with limited supervision. Judgment and discretion in working with highly confidential information are also critical. For placement on a U.S.-based Latin American team, relevant language skills and cultural knowledge are essential. Candidates should have a minimum GPA of 3.2.

Associate (Graduate)

We seek candidates who are highly motivated, assertive and skilled communicators, with the capacity to develop and manage client relationships. We also seek individuals with advanced quantitative and analytical skills who have an extensive knowledge of, and passion for, the financial markets. For placement on a U.S.-based international team, relevant language skills and cultural knowledge are essential.

Please describe your summer internships.

Summer Analyst (Undergraduate)

As a Private Banking summer intern, you attend a focused orientation/training program on the private banking business that introduces you to strategy, products and business groups. You also participate in a senior speaker forum that provides further exposure to these areas. You will take part in a performance management process where you will set and monitor your goals and objectives throughout the summer. Over the course of the summer, a variety of networking events introduce you to other JPMorgan Chase lines of business. At the end of the 10-week program, you may be offered employment in the full-time analyst program based on our business needs and your summer performance.

You will support our integrated team as an analyst in a banking, product or investment role. Depending on your role, you will help devise customized financial strategies for existing or prospective clients, become an expert in a range of proprietary models, conduct research and analysis, and assist with product development. You will make a valuable contribution to a team providing integrated delivery of financial solutions.

Summer Associate (Graduate)

You get hands-on experience through three three-week assignments working primarily with bankers, global investment specialists and product specialists. You may focus on new business and on existing clients' overall relationship with the Private Bank to ensure that client needs are met across many spectrums, such as banking, lending, and trust and estate planning. Or, you may play a lead role in our investment dialogue with clients to ensure that the proper investment plan is created and executed to help our clients reach their wealth goals.

Throughout the summer, associates attend training classes, senior speaker series and networking events, all of which geared to increase your exposure to all aspects of the firm. You work with a dedicated program manager who provides guidance and feedback throughout the summer. The summer program is an ideal way to meet the people who make JPMorgan a success, to experience our unique culture and to learn about our full-time opportunities. Our summer associates become primary candidates for our full-time program.

Inside the Firm: Culture and Training

Please describe any formal training programs for employees.

Analyst (Undergraduate)

The analyst program immerses you in the Private Bank's business strategy, structure and values. During the five-week training program, you gain a broad knowledge of the business, and develop proficiency with our proprietary tools, models and systems. The final week of training provides analysts with role-specific training that helps prepare you to effectively work with your team. You also have a mentor, a more experienced JPMorgan Private Banking employee, with whom you can develop an insightful one-on-one relationship. A program manager is responsible for ensuring your continuing professional progress and for guiding you toward development opportunities that suit your long-term career interests. Once the three-year program is completed, analysts may pursue further education or other opportunities outside the firm. Based on the firm's business needs and individual performance, analysts may be promoted to associate and move on to more senior roles on a banking or product/investment team within JPMorgan Private Bank.

Associate (Graduate)

The associate program immerses you in the JPMorgan Private Bank's business strategy, structure and values. You gain a thorough understanding of our capabilities in wealth advisory, investments, and credit and lending. During the course of the program, you are expected to sharpen your client communication and service skills. Subsequently, you will have training opportunities at key junctures throughout your tenure at the firm

Compensation

Please describe compensation and other monetary benefits at your firm.

JPMorgan Private Bank offers highly competitive starting salaries for the analyst and associate program. Analysts and Associate are eligible to receive incentive compensation at the end of each review period.

401(k)

Full-time employees are immediately eligible to make before-tax contributions of up to 20 percent of benefits pay (up to the legal limit). Generally, if eligible, after one year of service, you'll receive dollar-for-dollar matching contributions from JPMorgan Chase on the first 5 percent of your benefits pay contributed each pay period.

Retirement

The Retirement Plan provides each eligible employee with a notional cash balance account. In general, after one year of service, your account will be credited on a monthly basis with pay credits equal to 3 to 9 percent of your benefits pay, up to the legal limit, based on your years of completed service.

Employee Stock Purchase

Employees are eligible to purchase JPMorgan Chase common stock at a 5 percent discount.

Diversity

Please describe any diversity hiring efforts in regards to women.

Throughout the course of the recruiting year, the Private Bank will participate in various women's panels, lunches or dinners on the campuses of our core schools.

Please describe any diversity hiring efforts in regards to minorities.

JPMorgan Private Bank has formal relationships with colleges and programs to source BA/BS and MBA students from diverse groups. The firm has formal recruiting relationships with Florida A&M University, Howard University, Morehouse College and Spelman College for undergraduate recruiting. For each school, the firm has a corporate team dedicated to creating a visible presence on campus and to developing strong relationships with students interested in business careers.

In the U.S., JPMorgan Chase works with INROADS and the Sponsors for Educational Opportunity (SEO) to source candidates for internships. The program offers paid summer internships for students of color who are interested in a career in financial services. Internships last for 10 weeks in each location and provide an opportunity for students to acquire work experience while developing important business skills. Upon successful completion of the internships, top seniors have an opportunity for full-time employment.

The Consortium for Graduate Study in Management is a group of 14 graduate schools of business dedicated to providing opportunities in management education to

African-Americans, Hispanic Americans and Native Americans seeking business careers. JPMorgan Chase works with the Consortium to attract and hire members.

JPMorgan Chase also works with the Robert A. Toigo Foundation by providing mentors and career opportunities. The Toigo Foundation is dedicated to increasing the number of African-American, Hispanic American and Asian-Americans in the wholesale financial services arena. It does this by providing financial assistance, mentoring and summer internships and job placement services to the top minority candidates in business schools around the country.

Additional Information

At JPMorgan Private Bank our mission is simple: "first-class business...in a first-class way."

In everything we do, in every relationship we have, excellence and integrity are the guiding principles. Excellence means 160 years of experience and the depth of knowledge that comes from solving the complexities of significant wealth, $25 million or more in net worth, day in and day out. We challenge this knowledge with the boldest, most innovative thinking of today.

Integrity means keeping our clients' interests front and center always. Whether they have made their wealth or inherited it, we will create a razor-sharp strategy for achieving our clients' goals. It all begins with an astute understanding of our clients' individual needs. We use a strategic advisory approach that looks at both sides of our clients' balance sheet and works towards understanding their values and goals. We leverage the firm's global expertise to construct a seamless and fully integrated wealth management solution.

We offer our clients the broadest and deepest set of capabilities industry wide, encompassing investing, tax and estate planning, family office management, philanthropy, capital raising and special advisory services. In delivering these solutions we surround our clients with an integrated team of experts including a banker, investor, wealth advisor, fiduciary specialist and credit specialist, as well as partners in philanthropy, art advisory, insurance and family governance.

Underscoring our leadership position, we were named the No. 1 Private Bank for ultra-high-net-worth individuals by *Euromoney* in January 2006, and the Top Private Banking Team by *US Banker*, in its Annual Performance Ranking, in January 2006. We have relationships with over 40 percent of the individuals on the Forbes

Wealthiest Americans list (*Forbes*, 2005), and are the largest private bank in the U.S., with nearly $200 billion in assets under management, and the third largest in the world, with over $310 billion in assets under management.

Lazard Private Client Group

30 Rockefeller Plaza
New York, NY 10020
Phone: (212) 632-6000
www.lazardnet.com

EMPLOYMENT CONTACT

E-mail: LAMRecruiting@
Lazard.com

See careers at
www.lazard.com

Firm Chairman: Bruce Wasserstein
Firm CEO: Bruce Wasserstein
Firm Type: Public Company
2005 Total Firm Revenue (Worldwide): $1.36 billion
2005 Total Firm Net Income (Worldwide): $172.3 million
No. of Employees (Firmwide): 2,200
No. of Office Locations (Firmwide): 29
No. of Office Locations (Asset Management): 11
No. of Office Locations (Private Client Group): 1

Hiring Process

Recruiting

Undergrad: Where does your firm annually recruit?

• *Ivy League schools:* Columbia University, Harvard University, Princeton University, Yale University

• *Public state schools:* UC Berkeley, University of Illinois, University of Michigan, University of Virginia,

• *Private schools:* Claremont McKenna, Georgetown University, Northwestern University, Howard University, Stanford University, University of Chicago, Wellesley College

• *Other:* McGill University

Visit Vault at **www.vault.com** for insider company profiles, expert advice, career message boards, expert resume reviews, the Vault Job Board and more.

VAULT CAREER LIBRARY   165

Grad: Where does your firm annually recruit?

• *MBA programs:* Columbia Business School, Wharton School of Business (UPenn), Berkeley Haas School of Business, Harvard Business School, Stanford Graduate School of Business, University of Chicago Graduate School of Business

Hiring

What are the position titles for new hires coming out of undergrad? Out of grad school?

Undergrad: analyst; Grad: associate

Does your firm offer summer internships?

Yes. Undergrads join as summer analysts, graduates as summer associates.

Legg Mason Wealth Management

100 Light Street Baltimore, MD 21202-1099 Phone: (877) 534-4627 www.leggmason.com **EMPLOYMENT CONTACT** See "careers" at ww.leggmason.com	**Firm Chairman & CEO**: Raymond Adams Mason **Firm Type:** Public Company **2005 Private Wealth Management Revenue (Worldwide):** $568 million **2006 Total Firm Revenue (Worldwide):** $2.6 billion **2006 Total Firm Net Income (Worldwide):** $1.1 billion **No. of Employees (Firmwide):** 5,580 **No. of Office Locations (Worldwide):** 136

Hiring Process

Recruiting

Candidates can search for specific job opportunities and apply online. The corporate headquarters in Baltimore recruits for domestic positions located in Baltimore, Md., Stamford, Conn., New York, N.Y., and San Francisco, Calif.

Hiring

What are some of the requirements for jobs?

Legg Mason recruits the best and brightest individuals to join our firm. The firm welcomes staff from a wide range of backgrounds and skill levels, and provides them with the opportunity to team with world-class colleagues in an environment that fosters excellence and best practices in all of its endeavors.

Individuals who exhibit integrity, a strong work ethic and a desire to contribute to the growth and success of our firm are recruited through a wide range of methods. Once they join Legg Mason, we continue to support their professional development with a comprehensive series of internal programs and access to our mentoring program.

Compensation

Please describe compensation and other monetary benefits at your firm.

Employees are eligible for tuition reimbursement, a 401(k) savings plan and the employee stock purchase plan.

Please describe other perks.

The firm offers employees a discount legal services plan, flexible spending accounts for health and commuter expenses, paid time off and an employee referral bonus plan.

Diversity

Legg Mason promotes a diverse culture through recruitment and retention programs, as well as ongoing training and mentoring.

Additional Information

Legg Mason takes a client-centered approach to comprehensive wealth management by providing objective advice, investment management, strategic transactions and trust services to wealthy individuals, families, businesses, private foundations, charities and other nonprofit entities. The wealth management team focuses the collective expertise of Legg Mason's wealth management, asset management and trust disciplines on crafting guidance tailored to meet the specific needs and objectives of high-net-worth clients.

Lehman Private Investment Management

<table>
<tr><td>

745 Seventh Avenue
30th Floor
New York, 10019
Phone: (212) 526-7000
Fax: (212) 526-8766
www.lehman.com

**EMPLOYMENT
CONTACT**

Kim Harounian
Private Investment
Management Associate
Recruiting, U.S.
399 Park Avenue, 6th Floor
New York, NY 10022
E-mail:
pim.associate@lehman.com
www.lehman.com/careers/
main.htm

</td><td>

Firm Chairman & CEO: Richard S. Fuld Jr.
Firm Type: Public Company
2005 Private Investment Management Net Revenue (Worldwide): $903 million
2005 Total Firm Net Revenue (Worldwide): $14.6 billion
2005 Total Firm Net Income (Worldwide): $3.2 billion
No. of Employees (Firmwide): 22,919
No. of Office Locations (Worldwide): 47

</td></tr>
</table>

Hiring Process

Recruiting

The private investment management division recruits from MBA programs at Columbia, Cornell, Dartmouth, Duke, Harvard, MIT, NYU and Northwestern. Recruiting contacts for each college are listed on the campus recruiting page of the firm's web site.

In addition to campuses, where else does your firm recruit for employees?

Experienced hires interested in positions in the U.S. can e-mail a resume to humanresources.us@lehman.com.

Visit Vault at **www.vault.com** for insider company profiles, expert advice, career message boards, expert resume reviews, the Vault Job Board and more.

VAULT CAREER LIBRARY   169

Hiring

What are the position titles for new hires coming out of undergrad? Out of grad school?

For graduates with an advanced degree, the firm offers a small, highly customized program to maximize your individual potential. You begin your full-time career with three months of intensive training in New York. This commences with a comprehensive capital markets course that covers a variety of topics, including stock and bond analysis as well as an overview of the major capital markets instruments and businesses. During this time you will also gain exposure to many aspects of the firm through a series of business presentations, lectures and interactive projects.

Next, you will receive in-depth training on our investment management division's platform, products and capabilities. The final component of the program is designed to build impressive presentation and sales skills—and is taught by our most senior investment advisers. You will also receive training for the Series 7 and Series 63 registration exams.

Following the course, you will travel to your assigned job location where you will join your private investment team, assisting clients with long and short-term decisions regarding investment strategies and asset allocations. Here, you will use your entrepreneurial skills and enthusiasm for the markets to generate the knowledge to sell the firm's investment products. It is a steep learning curve, but we will team you with experienced investment team representatives as you build a high-net-worth client base. Throughout, you will benefit from a clear path of opportunity for career growth.

What are some of the requirements for jobs?

For the investment management group, the firm seeks candidates with an MBA or PhD (or promotion through the analyst stream) and a record of strong academic achievement, leadership experience and evidence of initiative. Candidates should also have distinctive problem-solving skills and strong professional presence combined with self confidence and maturity. The firm seeks applicants who have refined written and verbal communication skills, leadership potential, initiative and the ability to contribute to a team-based environment. Where experience dictates, solid technical knowledge of banking functions are also required.

Please describe your summer internships.

Candidates with an advanced degree can apply to the summer associate program. The 10-week program begins with one week of training followed by a three-week rotation with a private investment team in the New York office. Associates spend the remaining six weeks rotating through different private investment teams in their assigned branch office location. During these rotations, you will be exposed to the typical workflow of an investment representative. Typical projects include conducting research, compiling relevant market data and client data, creating sales presentations and attending client meetings.

Summer associates benefit from detailed feedback at the end of the first rotation in New York—and then again at the end of the 10-week program. You will also enjoy extensive contact with the firm's professionals at all levels through group events, informal functions and the leadership lecture series delivered by senior management. This feedback process prepares, determined, talented summer hires for permanent job offers in private investment management.

The division looks upon the summer associate program as a primary source for hiring full-time associates. So we strongly encourage all those interested in full-time roles to apply to the summer program.

Inside the Firm: Culture and Training

Please describe the corporate culture at your firm.

At the heart of Lehman Brothers' success is a distinctive culture built on teamwork. We encourage a flat, open structure that breaks down barriers between internal divisions, draws teams and business areas together, and releases the enterprise and energy of individuals.

This entrepreneurial, collaborative environment is integral to our "One Firm" approach to client satisfaction. We are able to offer clients the expertise of the entire firm, because every area of the business is united by a collegiate approach and the highest standards of integrity.

Please describe any scholarship programs at your firm.

The tuition reimbursement program provides a special benefit for employees who demonstrate effort, skill and dedication to their jobs and the firm. Managers may nominate and sponsor individuals who wish to further their education and enhance their knowledge and capabilities. The firm will reimburse certain courses taken by employees with manager's approval.

The firm also sponsors a part-time MBA program through an affiliation with New York University Stern School of Business. Employees from all divisions are

Visit the Vault Finance Career Channel at **www.vault.com/finance** — with insider firm profiles, message boards, the Vault Finance Job Board and more.

VAULT CAREER LIBRARY   **171**

nominated to apply and pursue their MBA degree while continuing employment at Lehman Brothers.

Compensation

Please describe compensation and other monetary benefits at your firm.

The Lehman Brothers Holdings Savings Plan is a 401(k) plan that provides an easy and convenient way to save for retirement. Lehman Brothers Bank also provides residential mortgages loans to qualified Lehman Brothers' employees under the Lehman Brothers Employee Mortgage Program. A wide variety of fixed and adjustable rate residential mortgages are available, for purchase or refinancing of residential properties located in the U.S.

Please describe other perks.

Lehman Brothers has negotiated discounts with a wide variety of vendors to provide employees with special rates at recreational, cultural and retail facilities. The firm also offers access to backup child care.

Diversity

Please describe any diversity hiring efforts in regards to minorities.

Chaired by the firm's co-chief operating officer, the global diversity council helps to shape corporate strategy on diversity issues. It also works with the firm's business leaders, in addition to the divisional and regional councils, to develop diversity plans and accountability measures around recruiting, retention and development.

Additional Information

Private investment management provides comprehensive investment, wealth advisory and capital markets execution services for high-net-worth individuals and businesses, leveraging all the resources of the firm. Business groups include investment management, portfolio advisory, wealth advisory, Lehman Brothers Trust Companies, capital advisory and the institutional client group.

Lydian Wealth Management

2600 Tower Oaks Boulevard,
Suite 300
Rockville, MD 20852
Phone: (301) 770-6300
Toll Free: (800) 251-9531
Fax: (301) 770-1408
www.lydianwealth.com

EMPLOYMENT CONTACT

Phone: (866) 272-2265
E-mail: jobs@lydian.com

See "careers" at
www.lydianwealth.com

Chairman, Lydian Trust Company:
Rory A. Brown
**President, Lydian Wealth
Management:** Andrew Putterman
CEO, Lydian Trust Company: Rory
A. Brown
Firm Type: Subsidiary of Lydian
Trust Company.
**No. of Office Locations
(Worldwide):** 11

Hiring Process

Lydian Wealth Management aims to be "perceived … as the premier wealth management firm in the world." To that end, the company rates building "intellectual capital" in the corporate environment among their top goals in hiring. Success-oriented, teamworking candidates with the highest standards will find "long-term personal satisfaction" at LWM.

Compensation

Please describe compensation and other monetary benefits at your firm.

The firm offers "competitive salaries, medical and dental insurance, 401(k), vacation, sick and personal days, and paid holidays"

Visit Vault at **www.vault.com** for insider company profiles, expert advice,
career message boards, expert resume reviews, the Vault Job Board and more.

VAULT CAREER LIBRARY   173

Diversity

"Lydian Wealth Management is an equal opportunity employer and does not discriminate on the basis of race, color, sex, religion, sexual orientation, national origin, marital status, age, handicap or veteran status."

Additional Information

Lydian Wealth Management services clients with assets of $10+ million. Because compensation is not based on commission or the collection of fees from other firms, LWM claims to provide their clients with a unique "true third-party objectivity," free of ulterior motives.

Mellon Private Wealth Management

One Mellon Center
Pittsburgh, PA 15258
Phone: (412) 234-5000
Fax: (412) 234-9495
www.mellon.com

**EMPLOYMENT
CONTACT**

E-mail: info@mellon.com
www.mellon.com/careers/index.
html

Firm Chairman & CEO: Robert P.
(Bob) Kelly
Firm Type: Public Company
**2005 Total Firm Revenue
(Worldwide):** $4.7 billion
**2005 Total Firm Net Income
(Worldwide):** $782 million
**No. of Employees (Private
Wealth):** 60 offices in 14 U.S.
states
No. of Employees (Firm-wide):
16,700
**No. of Office Locations
(Worldwide):** 98

Hiring Process

Where else does your firm recruit for employees (job postings, web sites, other firms, etc.)?

The career page of the firm's web site maintains a searchable database of job opportunities.

Candidates are invited to submit a resume through an online form, which can be used to apply to specific positions of interest. Mellon also recruits at various job fairs and events; a current recruiting calendar is on the career page of the web site. The web site also lists specific recruiting locations throughout the U.S., the U.K. and Ireland. The events calendar can be found at: www.mellon.com/careers/recruitingevents.html.

Please describe your summer internships.

Mellon's global internship program provides opportunities for college and high school students to map out career paths by gaining hands-on experience, skills and knowledge. The internship exposes students to the training, mentoring and networking opportunities needed to facilitate the transition from school to full-time employment. Participants in the global internship program work closely with a mentor who assists in navigating through the experience.

Inside the Firm: Culture and Training

Please describe any scholarship programs at your firm.

The tuition assistance program, available to all full- and part-time benefited employees, reimburses tuition according to the grade received for business/job related degrees or courses required for business/job related degrees. Full-time employees are eligible for $5,000 in reimbursements per calendar year. Part-time benefited employees are eligible for $2,500 in reimbursements per calendar year.

Compensation

Please describe compensation and other monetary benefits at your firm.

The Mellon 401(k) plan allows employees to contribute, on a pre-tax basis, from 1 percent to 75 percent of their eligible semi-monthly base pay. Mellon will match $.65 in Mellon Financial Corporation Common Stock for every $1 contributed (up to 6 percent) by participants. Participants are fully vested after completing three years of service. The firm also offers a pension plan at no cost. Employees are fully vested after five years of service.

Please describe other perks.

Mellon offers flex vacation—the opportunity to purchase additional vacation time in order to balance your work and family responsibilities. In addition, backup child care, sick child care reimbursement, adoption leave, educational seminars and flexible work arrangements are some of the benefits available to employees. The firm's wellness program offers on-site blood drives, flu shots, tai chi classes and yoga classes, as well as discounts to a nationwide network of health and fitness facilities.

Diversity

Please describe any diversity hiring efforts in regards to women.

Mellon's recruiting efforts are focused on identifying, attracting and retaining diverse candidates as part-time and full-time employees and interns. The firm recruits at women's events throughout the year, such as the Pennsylvania Governor's Conference for Women.

Please describe any diversity hiring efforts in regards to minorities.

The firm recruits at a variety of minority association events, including the National Black MBA conference and career fair.

The firm's Pittsburgh-based Black/African-American Affinity Network's mission is to share information that will help to enhance business acumen, coaching, community involvement and networking for black/African-American employees. The Black/African-American Affinity Network is open to all employees. The group works with human resources to engage members in Mellon programs and networks. It also supports recruitment and retention efforts of black and African-American qualified candidates and incumbent employees.

Among the business objectives of the Black/African-American Affinity Network are to gather employees who are interested in helping to enhance business acumen, coaching, community involvement and networking for black/African-American employees and to sponsor career development and coaching opportunities for those employees.

Another group, MORE Affinity Network, works to enhance the sharing and understanding of the myriad cultures Mellon employees represent, while promoting an inclusive environment, relationship-building and mentoring for its members. MORE works with members of Mellon Human Resources and other organizations to enhance opportunities for professional development and diversity initiatives.

Please describe any diversity hiring efforts in regards to gays and lesbians.

PRISM is the firm's affinity group that promotes and supports an environment at Mellon in which all gay, lesbian, bisexual and transgender (GLBT) employees are fully included in all aspects of corporate life, including advancement opportunities, support, mentoring and other issues vital to maintaining Mellon's commitment to becoming the employer of choice.

Visit the Vault Finance Career Channel at **www.vault.com/finance** — with insider firm profiles, message boards, the Vault Finance Job Board and more.

VAULT CAREER LIBRARY   **177**

Through educational, charitable and social activities, and together with our supporters, PRISM strives to meet the specific needs of Mellon's GLBT community, including the promotion of an environment where employees are welcomed, accepted and fully integrated. As members of both the Mellon and GLBT communities, PRISM also seeks to identify and provide opportunities to successfully bridge those communities, recognizing that these bridges encourage growth in business and personal lives.

Additional Information

Mellon is a national private wealth leader, providing wealth management, investment management and financial management services to individuals, families, family offices, entrepreneurs, professionals, charitable giving programs, endowments and foundations. Private wealth management offers investment and wealth management services to individuals and families with $1 million or more of investable assets as well as specialized services for family offices, endowments and foundations.

Merrill Lynch Global Private Client

4 World Financial Center 250 Vesey Street New York, NY 10080 Tel (212) 449-1000 Fax: (212) 449-9418 www.ml.com **EMPLOYMENT** **CONTACT** See "careers" at ww.ml.com	**Chairman & CEO:** E. Stanley O'Neal **Firm Type:** Public Company **2005 Private Wealth Management Net Revenue:** $10.7 billion **2005 Total Firm Revenue:** $47.7 billion **2005 Total Firm Net Income:** $5.1 billion **No. of Employees (Private Wealth):** 33,000 **No. of Employees (Firmwide):** 56,000 **No. of Office Locations (Worldwide):** 900

Hiring Process

Recruiting

Experience hires and new graduates can search for positions and apply directly through the firm's web site.

Hiring

What are the position titles for new hires coming out of undergrad? Out of grad school?

New hires from an undergrad program enter the global private client analyst program, a two-year leadership and development program in various business areas throughout the global private client group. After training, new hires are assigned to one of six core functional areas (private banking and investment, global banking, marketing, investment and wealth management, retirement or direct services) in New York City; Princeton, N.J.; Hopewell, N.J.; or Jersey City, N.J.

New MBA hires enter the global private client associate program. Associates receive a two-year assignment to one of the six core areas of the group and work in one of the firm's offices in New York City; Princeton, N.J; Jersey City, N.J; or Hopewell, N.J.

Please describe the hiring process at your firm.

Students typically submit applications from September to December, and the firm extends offers from November to March. Students are also welcome to search the experienced and entry-level job postings for appropriate open positions when they are nearing graduation and will be available for employment.

What are some of the requirements for jobs?

For graduates with a BA degree, all majors are accepted, and a minimum 3.2 GPA is required. Candidates should have at least one corporate work experience, preferably an internship in financial services. A background of diverse extracurricular activities and leadership roles is also desired. The firm looks for candidates with sharp quantitative skills, exceptional verbal and presentation skills, interpersonal abilities and an aptitude for creative problem solving. To be a successful candidate, you must show a commitment to a career in financial services, display initiative and leadership, demonstrate professionalism and integrity and have the motivation to achieve excellence.

For applicants with a graduate degree, requirements are a recent MBA or MBA/JD dual degree and a strong record of academic achievement. A minimum of three years of significant experience in financial services or related area between bachelor's and graduate degrees is required. The firm also looks for demonstrated leadership and managerial or supervisory experience, including extracurricular activities. Candidates should possess polished verbal and written communication skills plus outstanding presentation skills. In addition, candidates should be proficient in technology and have the ability to lead, support and motivate people. Certain personal traits make successful candidates in this group, a passion for the financial markets and a highly developed aptitude for quantitative and analytical thinking are necessary. It is also important that candidates have an entrepreneurial mind-set, enthusiasm, energy and are adaptable and results-oriented.

For financial advisor positions, three types of candidates are considered: experienced financial advisors, other professionals and those transitioning from the military. For experienced financial advisors, Merrill Lynch can enhance your career by offering a breadth of products and services unmatched in the industry and, with it, unparalleled opportunities to build and grow your practice. If you are an experienced professional in sales, or an attorney, banker or other professional considering a new career in the field of financial advising, we provide you with the training, the management resources and the team-based structure to grow your business quickly. If you are transitioning from the military and considering a career in financial services, we provide you with the training and the resources to get started in a new profession.

Please describe your summer internships.

The firm offers 10-week summer internships.

For MBA students, the private client summer associate program is a 10-week assignment that provides exposure to leadership roles in the private client business. Interns will attend an orientation for an introduction to Merrill Lynch and the global private client group (GPC). Interns have a chance to interact with senior management in the group and to network with peers in other programs. A highlight of the program is the summer senior speakers series, formal presentations by the heads of each of Merrill Lynch's principal business groups.

The private client analyst arogram is the 10-week summer program for undergraduate students. Over the course of the summer, interns receive extensive formal training that includes an introduction to Merrill Lynch and a thorough overview of the GPC business. Each intern is assigned a mentor and will receive formal performance evaluation at the middle and end of summer. Interns get the chance to interact with GPC management and network with other peers.

Interns are assigned to one of six core functional areas of the global private client business: private banking and investment, global banking, marketing, investment and wealth management, retirement and direct services. These central areas create and deliver products and services that support financial advisors who work with individual clients and families in branch offices.

Inside the Firm: Culture and Training

Please describe any scholarship programs at your firm.

The firm offers financial support for full-time employees who wish to pursue formal education relevant to their professional development (maximum annual reimbursement is $8,000).

Visit the Vault Finance Career Channel at **www.vault.com/finance** — with insider firm profiles, message boards, the Vault Finance Job Board and more.

V/\ULT CAREER LIBRARY   **181**

Please describe any formal training programs for employees.

New hires in the global private services group attend a firm wide orientation program and the institutional core training program, which provides an overview of financial markets and business skills. After orientation, analysts receive private client customized training on global markets products, services, work practices and transactions from origination to execution, if applicable to your functional area placement. Over the course of training, analysts develop analytical, marketing, communications, listening and interpersonal skills. The firm also offers preparation for the Series 7 and Series 66 licensing exams, if appropriate for the position. After training, analysts are placed in a four-week assignment in a U.S. branch office to learn first-hand about the sales organization and the role of financial advisors and to analyze branch office profitability and productivity. During training, quarterly business projects are assigned to expose analysts to other private client groups.

Compensation

Please describe compensation and other monetary benefits at your firm.

Merrill Lynch offers a 401(k) savings and investment plan and retirement program, and employee stock purchase plan and discounts on Merrill Lynch financial products and services.

Please describe other perks.

As part of the benefits package, employees receive dollars each month for a variety of expenses, (including parking fees and railroad, bus and subway fares), adoption planning and assistance, access to on-site and near-site fitness centers and a variety of child care assistance. The firm also offers scholarship programs for children of employees.

To support community involvement, employee gifts to eligible nonprofit organizations matched dollar for dollar when employee contributes gifts of $50 or more for a total yearly match of $1,500. Employees who volunteer with nonprofit organizations can receive grants of $100 to $1,000 for the organization's projects in which they have a direct role.

Diversity

Please describe any diversity hiring efforts in regards to minorities.

The firm emphasizes identifying candidates early in their college careers for summer internships and eventually for full-time positions following graduation. Merrill Lynch works with a number of organizations that help source outstanding college students. The firm has developed strong working relationships with Sponsors for Educational Opportunity (SEO), Capital Chances and historically black colleges such as Howard, Morehouse and Spelman. In addition, the firm partners with the following programs that expose high school students to the business world and help prepare them for future employment through the LEAD program.

The Merrill Lynch fellowship program awards merit-based fellowships to African-American, Native American, Hispanic and female students interested in financial services and entering graduate business school. The fellowship offers full tuition and fees for the first year of the MBA program, a paid summer associate position in global markets, investment banking, or capital markets at Merrill Lynch and full tuition and fees for the second year of the MBA program for those who complete the summer associate position and accept an offer for a full-time position at Merrill Lynch following graduation. To be eligible to apply, students must be accepted to enter the MBA program at Chicago, Columbia, Darden, Harvard, Kellogg, Stern or Wharton. Students must also be nominated by the school's office of admissions.

The firm's partnership with diversity organizations and participation in other sourcing activities help identify and build relationships with MBA candidates. In addition to the fellowship program for women and minority students, Merrill participates in the following programs and activities: Toigo Foundation, Consortium for Graduate Study in Management, the National Black MBA Conference, the National Society for Hispanic MBAs and many campus affinity groups.

Merrill Lynch offers several awards to students at Howard University, Morehouse College and Spelman College. Receipt of the scholarship is contingent on acceptance of a 10-week summer internship offer at Merrill Lynch.

Additional Information

Merrill Lynch's global private client (GPC) group provides advice-based wealth management services and products to individual clients and businesses. The largest portion of the GPC group's business is offered through the advisory division, where

Visit the Vault Finance Career Channel at **www.vault.com/finance** — with insider firm profiles, message boards, the Vault Finance Job Board and more.

VAULT CAREER LIBRARY　**183**

services are delivered by Merrill Lynch financial advisors through a global network of branch offices. Merrill has more than 15,000 financial advisors in nearly 700 offices around the world.

GPC serves the needs of high-net-worth individuals and small- to mid-sized business owners. Nearly two-thirds of assets under management come from relationships with clients who have investable assets of $1 million or more. The firm also serves thousands of individuals through employee retirement plans administered and managed on behalf of corporations.

Support for financial advisors is provided by GPC's six core functional areas: private banking and investment, global banking, marketing, investment and wealth management, retirement and direct services. They deliver products and services for clients and marketing assistance for financial advisors.

GPC's offerings include commission and fee-based investment accounts, trust and generational planning, retirement services and insurance products. In 2005, GPC generated 41 percent of Merrill Lynch's net revenue and 28 percent of Merrill Lynch's pre-tax earnings. GPC's growth priorities include hiring additional financial advisors, client segmentation, annuitization of revenue through fee-based products, diversification of revenue through adding products and services, investments in technology and disciplined expansion into additional geographic areas globally.

Morgan Keegan Private Client Group

Morgan Keegan Tower Memphis, TN 38103 Phone: (901) 524-4100 www.morgankeegan.com **EMPLOYMENT CONTACT** E-mail: jobs@morgankeegan.com See "career opportunities" section of www.morgankeegan.com	**Chairman:** Allen B. Morgan, Jr. **CEO:** G. Douglas Edwards **Firm Type:** Subsidiary of Regions Financial **2005 Total Firm Revenue (Worldwide):** $810.25 million **2005 Total Firm Net Income (Worldwide):** $101.69 million **No. of Employees (Firmwide):** 3,400+ **No. of Office Locations (Worldwide):** 7 institutional offices; 280 offices total

Hiring Process

Hiring

What are the position titles for new hires coming out of undergrad? Out of grad school?

MBAs: associate positions.

Please describe the hiring process at your firm.

Applications accepted and offers made year-round.

What are some of the requirements for jobs?

Highly motivated candidates with strong analytical skills and who will work well with the senior managers. The firm looks for new hires who will mature into senior bankers with the company.

Does your firm offer summer internships?

Yes.

Compensation

Please describe compensation and other monetary benefits at your firm.

The firm matches part of the 401(k) contribution, and it issues options and restricted cash. There is also a deferred compensation plan. Stock options are available for senior VPs and up.

Please describe other perks.

Parking/transportation plan, tuition reimbursement, discounted gym memberships, and free counseling for employees and their families.

Morgan Stanley Private Wealth Management

<table>
<tr><td>

1585 Broadway
New York, NY 10036
Phone: (212) 761-4000
www.morganstanley.com

**EMPLOYMENT
CONTACT**

Diversity employment e-mail:
diversityrecruiting@morgan
stanley.com

See "careers" at
www.morganstanley.com

</td><td>

Chairman & CEO: John J. Mack
Firm Type: Public Company
**2005 Total Firm Revenue
(Worldwide):** $52.08 billion
**2005 Total Firm Net Income
(Worldwide):** $4.939 billion
**No. of Office Locations
(Worldwide):** 600
No. of Employees (Firmwide):
53,218

</td></tr>
</table>

Hiring Process

Recruiting

The firm recruits at numerous schools, including Columbia University, Harvard University, University of Pennsylvania, Johns Hopkins University, Williams College, New York University, University of California at Berkeley, University of Chicago, Kellogg School, Stanford University, among others.

Hiring

What are the position titles for new hires coming out of undergrad? Out of grad school?

Undergrad: analyst; Grad: associate.

Please describe the hiring process at your firm:

Campus recruitment, online application, late autumn/winter first-round interviews; subsequent full-day interviews and meetings.

Does your firm offer summer internships?

Summer analyst program (for undergrads), summer associate program (grads).

Visit Vault at **www.vault.com** for insider company profiles, expert advice, career message boards, expert resume reviews, the Vault Job Board and more.

VAULT CAREER LIBRARY   187

Inside the Firm: Culture and Training

Please describe any formal training programs for employees.

The firm runs a five-month private wealth management associate program (for graduate degree-holders), which prepares employees for securities industry certification exams, in addition to training in Morgan Stanley specifics.

Compensation

Please describe other perks.

The firm offers many perks, including child and elder care, employee counseling, referral services, health and fitness courses and facilities.

Diversity

Please describe any diversity hiring efforts in regards to women.

Morgan Stanley participates in women's career conferences at University of Chicago, Columbia, Harvard, Kellogg, Stanford, Stern and Wharton, as well as national organizations, such as Graduate Women in Business National Conference. The firm's Women in Technology program provides a two-year academic scholarship and a paid summer internship in Morgan Stanley's IT department during the summer prior to graduation to qualified female undergraduate students.

Please describe any diversity hiring efforts in regards to minorities.

The firm participates in minority career conferences at University of Chicago, Columbia, Harvard, Kellog, Stanford and Wharton, and also in national organizations such as MBA Jumpstart, National Association of Black Accountants, National Black MBA Association, National Society of Black Engineers, National Society of Hispanic MBAs Conference, Society of Hispanic Professional Engineers, Fuqua Black and Latino MBA Organization.

The firm also offers several scholarship programs:

• Morgan Stanley Fellowship offers scholarship money and paid summer internships for minority undergraduates.

• Morgan Stanley Richard B. Fisher Scholars Program is a two-year academic scholarship and paid internship in institutional securities and IT.

- Morgan Stanley MBA Fellowship provides scholarship money and summer internships for minority grad students.

- Diversity High School Internship Program offers paid summer internships for minority high school students.

Please describe any diversity hiring efforts in regards to gays and lesbians.

The firm sponsors the Reaching Out MBA Conference for gay, lesbian and transgender students.

Visit the Vault Finance Career Channel at **www.vault.com/finance** — with
insider firm profiles, message boards, the Vault Finance Job Board and more.

VAULT CAREER LIBRARY   189

Northern Trust Private Banking

50 South La Salle Street
Chicago, IL 60603
Phone: (312) 630-6000
www.ntrs.com

EMPLOYMENT CONTACT

See "careers" at
www.northerntrust.com

Chairman & CEO: William A. Osborne
Firm Type: Private Company
2005 Total Firm Revenue (Worldwide): $2.69 billion
2005 Total Firm Net Income (Worldwide): $584.4 million
No. of Employees (Firmwide): 9,008
No. of Office Locations (Worldwide): 84 nationwide.

Hiring Process

Hiring

What are the position titles for new hires coming out of undergrad? Out of grad school?

Starting every July, recent college grads enter the firm's GOLD Program for 15 to 18 months, after which there is the possibility of being hired as investment associate, associate wealth advisor, new business consultant, account manager, credit analyst, credit portfolio manager, private banker, business process analyst and other titles.

Please describe the hiring process at your firm.

The GOLD Program recruitment lasts from September to December.

What are some of the requirements for jobs?

Bachelor's degree in liberal arts or business, GPA of 3.0 or better is preferred, recent college graduate or up to two years of work experience in the financial services industry.

Please describe your summer internships.

Summer internships at the Chicago office include classes in delivering presentations, leadership and diversity awareness. Work includes contact with the division president, games, lunches, workshops and presentations by the higher-ups. A mentor is assigned to each intern.

Inside the Firm: Culture and Training

Please describe any formal training programs for employees.

GOLD Program Training includes orientation with senior employees in business strategies, four-month rotations within a career track, training with staff as well as outside experts in technology, and classes on leadership, executive writing, teamwork and presentation skills.

Compensation

Please describe compensation and other monetary benefits at your firm.

Medical, dental, vision and life insurance; matching 401(k); profit-sharing plan; dependent life insurance, accidental death and dismemberment insurance; and tuition reimbursement, among others.

Please describe other perks.

Educational assistance, fitness center (with trainers), wide-ranging family services (from adoption to bereavement).

Diversity

Northern Trust supports "total diversity." In the workplace, the firm provides "Diversity at Work" training.

Additional Information

Private banking at Northern Trust is a division of the personal financial services group for those with high-net wealth. Also included in PFS is the wealth management group, aimed at individuals or families with more than $75 million in assets.

Raymond James Financial
Private Client Group

880 Carillon Parkway St Petersburg, FL 33702 Phone: (727) 567-1000 Fax: (727) 573-8365 www.raymondjames.com **EMPLOYMENT CONTACT** See "careers" at www.raymondjames.com	**Chairman & CEO:** Thomas Alan James **Firm Type:** Public Company **2005 Private Wealth Management Revenue (Worldwide):** $1.39 billion **2005 Total Firm Revenue (Worldwide):** $2.16 billion **2005 Total Firm Net Income (Worldwide):** $151 million **No. of Employees (Firmwide):** 4,886 **No. of Office Locations (Worldwide):** 2,200

Hiring Process

Hiring

What are some of the requirements for jobs?

We look for creative thinkers with intelligence, strong academic background, enthusiasm and ambition, as well as interpersonal and analytical skills. We are looking for bright, energetic graduates and undergraduates with high integrity who share our commitment to a client-needs-driven business philosophy. As we believe a fulfilling life includes work, family, cultural, athletic and civic facets, we encourage you to share our "work, work, play" lifestyle. If you want to use your talents to assist corporations in raising capital or to aid investors in achieving their goals in a challenging environment, consider Raymond James as the place to productively employ your education, skills and energy.

Visit Vault at **www.vault.com** for insider company profiles, expert advice, career message boards, expert resume reviews, the Vault Job Board and more.

VAULT CAREER LIBRARY   193

Inside the Firm: Culture and Training

Please describe the corporate culture at your firm.

Raymond James prides itself on being a company that specializes in innovative investment and financial planning alternatives. Our associates and their commitment to client service remains the constant driving force behind our phenomenal growth. At Raymond James, great emphasis is placed on the individual role of each employee. All of our associates are on a first-name basis, senior management is accessible and strength is provided by our family atmosphere.

Because every employee fulfills a vital role in servicing clients and in contributing to the firm's overall success, we devote time and resources to nurturing personal growth. The firm also plans a variety of company-wide events each year, such as Breakfast with the Boss, when associates spend breakfast or lunch with CEO and Chairman Tom James every quarter. These meetings are a vital part of keeping our associates up to date on current corporate and industry events. Employees also participate in cultural awareness week, Halloween celebrations, charitable giving campaigns, support for the arts and Service 1st Suppers and Luncheons, an open forum with the CEO and chairman.

Please describe any scholarship programs at your firm.

If you want to pursue a higher education degree, we'll pay most tuition costs through our tuition assistance program. Work-related seminars, workshops and classes may also qualify for reimbursement.

Please describe any formal training programs for employees.

Raymond James University, our in-house educational program, offers industry, technology and leadership development courses throughout the year. Employees can earn company-recognized degrees while learning the latest strategies and technologies for getting ahead and providing the finest client service. Classes in accounting, operations, marketing and other areas are also offered to help you learn new skills outside your chosen field. These courses provide the building blocks necessary to embark on a different career at Raymond James.

RJU courses are taught at our international headquarters, located in St. Petersburg, Fla., and in Detroit. RJU uses cutting-edge technology and state-of-the-art training facilities, and is a very popular corporate benefit for all associates. If you work in one of our worldwide locations and cannot attend RJU, you can learn at your computer without ever leaving the office. Through our e-learning program, associates can take industry and computer courses from their own desks—at convenient times for them.

Compensation

Please describe compensation and other monetary benefits at your firm.

The firm offers a range of investment and profit-sharing opportunities. Through a profit sharing plan, Raymond James allocates a portion of profits into a general pool of money that is distributed to eligible employees. Vested funds are dispersed when the employee reaches a predetermined retirement age. Through the employee stock ownership plan shares of stock are allocated to eligible employees who can later cash in the vested portion of their portfolio when they retire. The matched 401(k) plan provides a way for employees to save for retirement. The employee stock ownership plan allows eligible employees to purchase Raymond James stock at a discount. A securities discount allows employees to pay less for trade transactions

Please describe other perks.

Employees receive discounts to area theme parks, sporting events, retail stores, restaurants, salons and health clubs and more. The Raymond James Travel Department assists employees with personal travel plans. Employees have access to on-site amenities including cafeterias, dry cleaning, shoe repair, ATMs, postal services and auto detailing. In addition, the Florida License on Wheels and Florida Blood Services on-campus visits several times throughout the year.

Diversity

Please describe any diversity hiring efforts in regards to women.

Raymond James is dedicated to an inclusive and diverse environment where differences are understood, respected and valued. Our commitment will enable us to successfully embrace the diverse markets we serve and capitalize on the talents of all our associates. Diversity is our pledge to the clients and associates of Raymond James Financial.

Visit the Vault Finance Career Channel at **www.vault.com/finance** — with
insider firm profiles, message boards, the Vault Finance Job Board and more.

VAULT CAREER LIBRARY   **195**

Additional Information

Through the firm's four broker/dealer subsidiaries (Raymond James & Associates and Raymond James Financial Services in the U.S., Raymond James Ltd. in Canada, and Raymond James Investment Services in the U.K.) and two trust companies, the firm's private client group provides financial planning services, securities and insurance brokerage, cash management and trust services to more than 1.3 million accounts. The group is comprised of 4,886 advisors who affiliate as either traditional employees, quasi-independent employees, independent contractors, independent RIAs or employees in local banks or credit unions. We also provide clearing services for 39 corresponding firms with an additional 633 advisors.

Royal Bank of Canada Global Private Banking

200 Bay Street Toronto, Ontario Canada Phone: (416) 974-5151 Fax: (416) 955-7800 www.rbcprivatebanking.com **EMPLOYMENT CONTACT** See "careers" at www.rbc.com	**Chairman:** David P. O'Brien **Firm CEO:** Gordon M. Nixon **Firm Type:** Public Company **2005 Private Wealth Management Revenue (Worldwide):** $2.3 billion (approx.) **2005 Total Firm Revenue (Worldwide):** $12.55 billion **2005 Total Firm Net Income (Worldwide):** $2.34 billion **No. of Employees (Private Wealth):** 2,000 **No. of Employees (Firmwide):** 69,000 **No. of Office Locations (Worldwide):** 30

Hiring Process

Recruiting

In Canada, the fimr recruits at numerous universities, including Western University, McGill University, Concordia University, University of Alberta, Queens University, University of Toronto, University BC, HEC, University of New Brunswick, University of Ottawa, McMaster University, University of Sask, York University, University of Calgary, University of Victoria, Sauder School of Business, Dalhousie University, Simon Fraser University, University Fredericton and Memorial University of Newfoundland.

Hiring

What are the position titles for new hires coming out of undergrad? Out of grad school?

The firm offers six- to 12-month internships through its Career Edge program (www.careeredge.ca). MBA graduates join as financial analysts in the finance management development program.

Please describe the hiring process at your firm.

Candidates go through a behavioural interview (i.e., past performance in a similar situation) with professional recruiter, and subsequent interviews with other staff.

Inside the Firm: Culture and Training

Please describe the corporate culture at your firm.

Integrity and treating clients and each other well are top priorities at RBC.

Please describe any scholarship programs at your firm.

The following are scholarships the firm offers:

• Aboriginal Student Awards Program

• McGill University's Rowland C. Frazee—Post Graduate Scholarship

• Queen's University's Allan R. Taylor Scholarship and W. Earle McLaughlin Scholarship

• Dalhousie University's Rowland C. Frazee Undergraduate Scholarship

• Canadian Merit Scholarship Foundation

• Lester B. Pearson College of the Pacific

• Royal Winnipeg Ballet—Awards of Excellence Scholarships

• Shad Valley

• Canadian Aboriginal Arts Foundation

• Harry Jerome Scholarship Funds (Undergraduate Scholarships)

• RBC Medical & Dental Student Scholarship

Please describe any formal training programs for employees.

The firm holds orientation and on-boarding programs.

Please describe any ongoing or other training programs for employees.

The firm holds e-learning, career development programs, accreditation program, external seminars and conferences.

Diversity

The firm holds Business Excellence Through Diversity workshops for managers, as well as Diversity in Action and Building Cross-Cultural Compentence classes. Additionally, interns are hired from Ability Edge (graduates with disabilities).

Please describe any diversity hiring efforts in regards to women.

Closing the Gender Gap is a report regarding workplace behavior distributed to employees. The firm also supports and occasionally hires from the Calgary Immigrant Women's Association and Women's Association of Financial Counsellors

Please describe any diversity hiring efforts in regards to minorities.

The firm recruits from the National Society of Hispanic MBAs, and supports the Minority Employee Association (U.S.) and the Royal Eagles and Royal Aboriginal Circle (Canada).

Please describe any diversity hiring efforts in regards to gays and lesbians.

RBC supports the Gay, Lesbian and Allied Dain Employees group (U.S.).

Visit the Vault Finance Career Channel at **www.vault.com/finance** — with
insider firm profiles, message boards, the Vault Finance Job Board and more.

V/\ULT CAREER LIBRARY   **199**

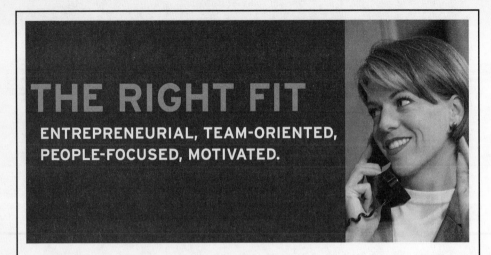

THE RIGHT FIT

ENTREPRENEURIAL, TEAM-ORIENTED, PEOPLE-FOCUSED, MOTIVATED.

The right fit. When it comes to your career, it can mean one that fits your personality, or maybe one that capitalizes on your talents or maximizes your skills. Or perhaps it's one that does all three—like a career as a Smith Barney Financial Advisor.

We're looking for a diverse group of people from a range of backgrounds to join us in a firm that is people-focused, entrepreneurial-based and growth-oriented, one that rewards individual initiative and team building. If this sounds like your goal, we may have the perfect fit for you here.

To find out more or to apply online, please visit www.smithbarney.com/recruiting

Smith Barney

787 Seventh Ave.
New York, NY 10019
Phone: (212) 492-6900
www.smithbarney.com

**EMPLOYMENT
CONTACT**

www.smithbarney.com/recruiting

Chairman & CEO, Citigroup Inc.: Chuck Prince
Firm Type: Division of Citigroup Inc.
2005 Private Wealth Management Revenue (Worldwide): $6.8 billion
2005 Total Firm Revenue (Worldwide): $86.3 billlion (Citigroup)
2005 Total Firm Net Income (Worldwide): $24.6 billion (Citigroup)
2005 Total Firm Net Income: $871 million (Smith Barney)
No. of Employees (Private Wealth): 13,414
No. of Employees (Firmwide): 275,000 (Citigroup)
No. of Office Locations (Worldwide): 624

Hiring Process

Recruiting

Experienced financial advisors can submit an application online through the Citigroup career web site. Candidates can search jobs, create a profile and submit a resume through the online Smith Barney Financial Advisor Career Center at: www.identifythebest.com/SmithBarneyws/home.asp.

Visit Vault at **www.vault.com** for insider company profiles, expert advice,
career message boards, expert resume reviews, the Vault Job Board and more.

VAULT CAREER LIBRARY   201

Hiring

What are some of the requirements for jobs?

For experienced professionals interested in a career in our global private client group there are opportunities in financial planning, advisory services, marketing and sales support staff. Ideal candidates are professionals with sales experience, bankers, attorneys and financial planners with five or more years of professional experience developing business. However, many financial advisors began without direct sales experience and from fields without a financial focus. We want people who have worked hard and have seen their hard work pay off—but who want more. Our selection process is careful and very thorough. Regardless of your background, you should be motivated, competitive, ambitious and have an entrepreneurial spirit. We believe this is the best way to build satisfaction for both the financial advisor and our clients. We want people who think outside the box—people with an intellectual hunger to find better ways of doing things, thinking strategically, working toward goals, searching for opportunities and leveraging them.

Inside the Firm: Culture and Training

Please describe the corporate culture at your firm.

Why do financial advisors stay with us for such a long time? A big part of the answer has to do with our entrepreneurial culture. We start with the premise that you know what's best for your business. Then we supply the tools, training and support you need. We don't expect you to sacrifice long-term relationships for short-term sales goals. We understand that relationship building is the cornerstone of a successful financial services business.

We help your clients stay your clients by allowing you to exceed expectations. Backed by the global strength of Citigroup, your clients will be able to choose from an array of strategies and services to suit each individual. It's no secret that when clients are satisfied, they stay with you. They also entrust you with more of their assets. At Smith Barney, we believe your client relationships will be stronger because your clients will see you as the source of ideas and creative strategies.

Please describe any formal training programs for employees.

Our 36-month paid training program is designed to give new employees the investment knowledge, business-building skills and confidence that will lead to success. The training begins on your first day in the branch, where you work under the direction and guidance of the branch manager. After completing the branch-based portion of training, you travel to our state-of-the-art facility in Hartford, Conn., where you experience intense training for three weeks.

New employees return to the branch to initiate production and additional training. Financial advisor associates who meet certain minimum performance requirements return to Hartford for a second advanced training session. Financial advisor associates who complete their first year in production at the top of their class will be invited to our New York City headquarters for advanced training and opportunities to meet senior Smith Barney and Citigroup executives.

Please describe any ongoing or other training programs for employees.

At Smith Barney, you can expand your role as trusted advisor to ultra high-net-worth clients with our private wealth management training and designation program. Through it, you'll become skilled at profiling clients, learning about their personal as well as their financial needs.

Compensation

Please describe compensation and other monetary benefits at your firm.

Eligible financial advisors also have the opportunity to participate in highly attractive benefits programs that are among the most competitive in our industry. The capital accumulation program enables you to elect to have a portion of your prospective compensation paid in the form of restricted shares of Citigroup common stock awarded at a 25 percent discount. The deferred compensation plan allows employees to choose to defer a portion of pre-tax earnings with either of two plans. The 401(k) plan enables associates to contribute up to 50 percent of pre-tax compensation and offers a wide variety of investment alternatives. Upon retirement, associates can participate in the franchise protection program. Retiring financial advisors in this program are eligible to receive commission splits (currently available in 35 states) up to a maximum of five years, from the accounts passed onto another financial advisor.

Diversity

Please describe any diversity hiring efforts in regards to women.

Smith Barney has special internal recruiting efforts for women and minorities. To achieve diversity goals, the firm is strengthening and expanding its relationships with top schools that have strong women and minority representation. The firm also hosts recruiting seminars for financial advisors around the country to attract a broad pool of talent.

Visit the Vault Finance Career Channel at **www.vault.com/finance** — with insider firm profiles, message boards, the Vault Finance Job Board and more.

VAULT CAREER LIBRARY   **203**

Additional Information

Smith Barney is the global private wealth management unit of Citigroup. It is a leading provider of comprehensive financial planning and advisory services to high-net-worth investors, institutions, corporations and private businesses, governments and foundations. With more than 13,000 financial consultants in some 624 offices, Smith Barney offers a full suite of investment services, including asset allocation, private investments and lending services, hedge funds, cash and portfolio management, as well as retirement, education and estate planning. The firm currently has more than 7.7 million client accounts, representing $1,015 billion in client assets.

Thomas Weisel Partners
Private Client Services

One Montgomery Tower One Montgomery Street San Francisco, CA 94104 Phone: (415) 364-2500 Fax: (415) 364-6295 E-mail: TWPInfo@tweisel.com www.tweisel.com	**Chairman & CEO:** Thomas Weisel **Firm Type:** Public Company **2005 Private Wealth Management Revenue (Worldwide):** $15.6 million **2005 Total Firm Revenue (Worldwide):** $256 million **2005 Total Firm Net Income (Worldwide):** -$7.1 million
EMPLOYMENT CONTACT Katie Baldino E-mail: jobs@tweisel.com Phone: (415) 364-2500 See "careers" at www.thomasweisel.com	**No. of Employees (Private Wealth):** 48 **No. of Employees (Firmwide):** 550 **No. of Office Locations (Worldwide):** 5

Hiring Process

Recruiting

Undergrad: The firm recruits on campuses such as Penn, NYU and Stanford. A complete recruiting calendar is available on the firm's web site. In addition to campus visits, Thomas Weisel also conducts off-campus recruiting from Berkeley, Brown, Carnegie Mellon, Chicago, Columbia, Dartmouth, Georgetown, Harvard, Michigan, Notre Dame, Princeton, USC, UT Austin, UVA and Yale.

Grad: The firm has on-campus MBA recruiting events at Tuck. The firm conducts off-campus recruiting from MBA programs at Chicago, Columbia, Duke, UC Berkeley, Harvard Business School, MIT, Michigan, NYU, Northwestern, Stanford, UCLA and Virginia.

Visit Vault at **www.vault.com** for insider company profiles, expert advice, career message boards, expert resume reviews, the Vault Job Board and more.

VAULT CAREER LIBRARY   205

Candidates from other schools can apply by sending a cover letter and resume to campusrecruiting@tweisel.com. In the e-mail, applicants should specify to which department they are applying. Job opportunities are also listed by department on the firm's web site, where candidates can directly e-mail an application for specific positions. Thomas Weisel also lists openings on various job search websites.

Hiring

What are some of the requirements for jobs?

TWP seeks to hire highly-motivated college graduates who are distinguished by their academic and extracurricular achievements and summer work experience. A background in quantitative coursework along with strong writing and communication skills are also required. Associate candidates should have an MBA or equivalent grad degree, prior investment banking experience as an analyst or associate and possess strong quantitative, communication and interpersonal skills.

Inside the Firm: Culture and Training

Please describe the corporate culture at your firm.

Associates have frequent contact with senior executives of publicly traded companies, as well as professionals at the nation's top institutional investment firms.

Please describe any mentoring programs at your firm.

Senior bankers train and mentor analysts on a broad variety of skills including analytics, financial accounting, project management, team management, client management and career management. Also, for those who decide to pursue an MBA after the analyst program, the senior professionals are actively involved in this process by providing business school recommendations and career advice. Because of the smaller size of project teams and the high level of interaction analysts often have with clients, many analysts have had corporate clients provide graduate school recommendations—another factor that distinguishes TWP from larger investment banks.

Please describe any formal training programs for employees.

Upon joining the firm, analysts and associates attend a three-week introductory training program in San Francisco. The first week is focuses on financial accounting and is taught by a graduate level business school professor. The final two weeks of the training program are taught by senior investment bankers in their various areas of product expertise. These sessions are focused on research, valuation and other analytical methodologies used for structuring and executing the firm's core banking products. Along with classroom presentations, analysts and associates work in teams to develop a mock IPO pitch and a mock M&A fairness opinion. These exercises are highly effective in preparing the new class for future assignments.

Please describe any ongoing or other training programs for employees.

Periodically, bankers organize lunch time training sessions around a topic, such as a recent transaction or an interesting structuring or accounting development. The discussions are lead by an expert peer and are focused on the analyst and associate ranks. These "peer-to-peer" sessions allow junior professionals to learn from their colleagues and develop client presentation skills in a low-risk environment. The firm also holds best practices workshops and industry teach-ins and panels.

Additional Information

Our private client services department offers brokerage and advisory services to high-net-worth individuals and cash management services to corporate clients. Our experienced professionals emphasize capital preservation through prudent planning and work closely with clients to customize solutions that address their individual needs. As of December 31, 2005, the aggregate value of assets in our client accounts was $9.2 billion. The 48-member group is managed by Shaugn Stanley and Jeff Handy, co-directors of the private client services department.

Visit the Vault Finance Career Channel at **www.vault.com/finance** — with insider firm profiles, message boards, the Vault Finance Job Board and more.

VAULT CAREER LIBRARY   **207**

Your exceptional talent drives our success. It starts with you.

Our employees are what make UBS a global financial powerhouse. Their ideas, skills and commitment to excellence are the bedrock of our success. So at UBS, we offer you a world of opportunities to enable you to achieve. Every one of our offices around the globe is built on the respect and support you need to meet your potential and help you to excel. To keep you inspired we provide the best training available. From day one, we value your skills and ambition.

It starts with you: **www.ubs.com/graduates**

UBS is an equal opportunity employer committed to diversity in its workplace. (M/F/D/V)

Wealth Management | Global Asset Management | Investment Bank

You & Us

 UBS

UBS Wealth Management

101 Park Avenue New York, NY 10178 www.ubs.com **EMPLOYMENT CONTACT** www.ubs.com/graduates	**Chairman:** Marcel Ospel **CEO:** Peter Wuffli **Firm Type:** Public Company **2005 Private Wealth Management Revenue (Worldwide):** CHF 4.2 billion **2005 Total Firm Revenue (Worldwide):** CHF 13.5 billion **2005 Total Firm Net Income (Worldwide):** CHF 39.9 billion **No. of Employees (Private Wealth):** 27,000 **No. of Employees (Firmwide):** 70,000+ **No. of Office Locations (Worldwide):** Located in 50 countries

Hiring Process

Recruiting

Undergrad: The firm recruits at University of Pennsylvania, Columbia, University of Chicago, University of Miami.

Grad: The firm recruits at Thunderbird.

Where else does your firm recruit for employees (job postings, web sites, other firms, etc.)?

Internal web site and referrals.

Hiring

What are the position titles for new hires coming out of undergrad? Out of grad school?

Graduate/analyst (undergrad), associate (MBA).

Visit Vault at **www.vault.com** for insider company profiles, expert advice, career message boards, expert resume reviews, the Vault Job Board and more.

VAULT CAREER LIBRARY   209

Please describe the hiring process at your firm.

Presentation, career fair, "target" event (focused on student organizations), three rounds of behavioral/analytical interviews with managers from the business.

What are some of the requirements for jobs (GPA, degree, personality, skills, etc.)?

GPA of 3.5 and above, strong analytical and communication/interpersonal skills.

Please describe your summer internships.

Ten-week internship paid bi-weekly. Competitive salary; work is dependent on the group that the intern is hired into.

Inside the Firm: Culture and Training

Please describe the corporate culture at your firm.

We strive for the development of a common culture—a culture of growth and performance. This is a critical and fundamental aspect for the success of our business.

As a business, we aim to offer independently minded, self-reliant people a platform on which to develop and realize their potential, and to create an environment in which individual performance receives the same recognition as a team's performance. Recognizing performance—by means of monetary and other incentives—lays the foundation for personal and professional development, and ensures that people are willing to go the extra mile.

Please describe any mentoring programs at your firm.

We have various mentoring programs throughout the firm aimed at various groups within the firm. All new hires through our graduate training program, for example, are assigned a mentor when they arrive at UBS.

Please describe any formal training programs for employees.

UBS offers an extensive training program as part of our graduate training program. The program varies in duration and content based on the specific business area to which you've been hired.

Please describe any ongoing or other training programs for employees.

People are our key asset to grow the business. Therefore we focus on driving and enabling talent development on all levels and in all businesses. We offer extensive training and development opportunities to all employees. Technical, key competency, managerial and leadership training courses are offered.

Compensation

Please describe compensation and other monetary benefits at your firm.

Salaries are competitive. Benefits are competitive.

Please describe other perks.

Competitive.

Hours

On average, how many hours do professionals work in the office per week?

Hours vary.

How often do they work on weekends?

Rarely.

Other comments on workload/hours:

Opportunity to travel extensively.

Diversity

Please describe any diversity hiring efforts in regards to women, minorities, and gays and lesbians.

We strive to hire diverse candidates reflecting gender, minorities and sexual orientation.

Visit the Vault Finance Career Channel at **www.vault.com/finance** — with insider firm profiles, message boards, the Vault Finance Job Board and more.

VAULT CAREER LIBRARY   **211**

Additional Information

When clients develop a relationship with UBS, they join forces with a global financial powerhouse delivering expertise in world markets and a wealth of banking experience built up over 140 years. With a culture of innovation, quality of service and demonstrated balance sheet strength, we are fully focused on our clients' needs and goals.

U.S. Bank Private Client Group

U.S. Bancorp Center
800 Nicollet Mall
Minneapolis, MN 55402
Phone: (651) 466-3000
www.usbank.com

**EMPLOYMENT
CONTACT**

See "careers" at
www.usbank.com

Chairman & CEO: Jerry A.
Grundhofer
Firm Type: Public Company
**2005 Total Firm Revenue
(Worldwide):** $13,133 Million
**2005 Total Firm Net Income
(Worldwide):** $4,489 Million
No. of Employees (Firmwide):
49,684

Hiring Process

Recruiting

The firm holds recruiting events in Minnesota, California, Georgia and Ohio. For details, check out the firm's careers web site.

Inside the Firm: Culture and Training

Please describe the corporate culture at your firm.

U.S. Bancorp emphasizes customer service above all, and looks for employees who will be dedicate themselves to this goal and to upholding the bank's high ethical standards regarding both treatment of customers and colleagues.

Please describe any ongoing or other training programs for employees.

Tuition reimbursement, financial training courses, development network for personal and professional development.

Visit Vault at **www.vault.com** for insider company profiles, expert advice, career message boards, expert resume reviews, the Vault Job Board and more.

VAULT CAREER LIBRARY 213

Compensation

Please describe compensation and other monetary benefits at your firm.

A 401(k) with immediate eligibility and company matching program, pension, reimbursement for medical, child care and parking

Please describe other perks.

U.S. Bank LifeWorks employee assistance program; earned and purchased vacation plans; adoption assistance reimbursement program; U.S. Bank HealthWorks program (nurse line, pregnancy programs, disease management self-care help); retiree health care, death, disability, life, health, vision and dental insurance; and transit plans.

Diversity

Please describe any diversity hiring efforts in regards to minorities:

U.S. Bancorp uses the services of the INROADS organization, which recruits students of color for pre-professional internships. Recruitment at National Black MBA Association 28th National Conference, National Society of Hispanic MBAs, and The National Association of Asian American Professionals National Convention.

U.S. Trust Wealth Management

11 West 54th Street New York, NY 10019 Phone: (212) 852-1000 www.ustrust.comE-mail: info@ustrust.com **EMPLOYMENT CONTACT** Mike Lowe recruiting2@ustrust.com See "careers" at www.ustrust.com	**CEO:** Peter K. Scaturro **Firm Type:** Subsidiary of The Charles Schwab Corporation **No. of Employees (Firmwide):** 2,300+ **No. of Office Locations (Worldwide):** 39

Hiring Process

Recruiting

On the U.S. Trust web site, interested candidates can view the list of open positions at U.S. Trust and apply for any position. Candidates can also search for open positions through Charles Schwab's career page at www.aboutschwab.com/careers. U.S. Trust also lists job openings on several job search web sites.

Inside the Firm: Culture and Training

Please describe the corporate culture at your firm.

U.S. Trust is one of the oldest and most respected wealth management and trust companies in America. We are committed to attracting, developing and retaining talented, intelligent and highly-motivated individuals. We expect our employees to be professional, well trained and dedicated to the highest standards of performance, quality, integrity and client service.

Our greatest asset is our people, and our objective is to build long-term relationships with them. They are essential to the accomplishment of our mission. We provide an atmosphere where employees can excel and grow, and superior achievement is rewarded.

Compensation

Please describe compensation and other monetary benefits at your firm.

We offer a competitive compensation package and an exceptional benefits program, which includes a defined benefit pension plan.

Additional Information

U.S. Trust's wealth management group serves individuals, business owners, corporate executives and families. We know how to deliver integrated plans utilizing an array of capabilities that encompass planning, investment management, trust services and private banking.

Wachovia Wealth Management

301 South College Street
Suite 4000
One Wachovia Center
Charlotte, NC 28288-0013
Phone: (704) 374-6161
www.wachovia.com

Wachovia Wealth
Management web site
www.wachovia.com/wealth

EMPLOYMENT CONTACT

Phone: (800) 386-4473
See the "careers" page of
www.wachovia.com

Chairman, President & CEO: G. Kennedy (Ken) Thompson
Firm Type: Public Company
2005 Private Wealth Management Revenue (Worldwide): $1.3 billion
2005 Total Firm Revenue (Worldwide): $26.1 billion
2005 Total Firm Net Income (Worldwide): $6.6 billion
No. of Employees (Private Wealth): 980
No. of Employees (Firmwide): 93,980
No. of Office Locations (Worldwide): 740 offices

Hiring Process

Hiring

Wachovia's selection processes differ from position to position, and are designed to effectively match an individual's knowledge, skills, interests and experiences to those needed for a particular position. During the process, a candidate may have a job preview, a structured behavioral interview and an assessment procedure. In-depth information about what to expect in the interview process and how to prepare can be found on the web site's career page in the interview section.

Visit Vault at **www.vault.com** for insider company profiles, expert advice, career message boards, expert resume reviews, the Vault Job Board and more.

VAULT CAREER LIBRARY   217

Inside the Firm: Culture and Training

Please describe any scholarship programs at your firm.

Wachovia's education reimbursement program is available to eligible employees for career-related classes.

Please describe any ongoing or other training programs for employees.

Wachovia's Learning Connection, an internal web site, is the point of access to a wide range of tools and resources that support ongoing learning and development. Employees can sign up for management essentials training, visit the library and explore online learning opportunities.

Compensation

Please describe compensation and other monetary benefits at your firm.

Employees can participate in a matched savings plan where the firm matches up to 6 percent of contributions, as well as a pension plan.

Please describe other perks.

Employees are eligible to receive special financial services such as free checking accounts, preferred interest rates on loans, discount traveler's checks and a free safety deposit box. Several of the firm's offices have on-site child care centers, and parents receive discount child care at some participating child care facilities. Flexible work options, such as job sharing, telecommuting and flexible hours, are available to employees. The firm's Time Away from Work program offers paid time off options in addition to vacation. Employees are also allowed up to four hours per month away from work to participate in volunteer activities.

Diversity

Please describe any diversity hiring efforts in regards to minorities.

Wachovia is an active participant in the INROADS internship program, which offers paid internships with Fortune 1000 companies for minority students.

Wachovia's Corporate Diversity Council is chaired by CEO Ken Thompson and includes a cross-section of individuals from across the company. The Corporate Diversity Council develops and maintains Wachovia's strategic plan for diversity and monitors the company's progress. The council meets quarterly to review status and recommend actions. The council's strategic plan supports our customer relationship, employee engagement and supplier diversity priorities

Additional Information

Wachovia Wealth Management manages $134.3 billion for clients around the world (as of March 31, 2006.) It provides financial advice, planning and integrated wealth management services to affluent and ultra-high-net-worth clients using a team-based approach. Business lines include private banking, personal trust, investment advisory services, charitable services, financial planning and Wachovia Insurance Services.

Wells Fargo Private Client Services/Private Banking

420 Montgomery Street
San Francisco, CA 94104
Phone: (866) 249-3302
www.wellsfargo.com

**EMPLOYMENT
CONTACT**

www.wellsfargo.com/employ
ment/working/

Chairman & CEO: Richard M. Kovacevich
Firm Type: Public Company
2005 Total Firm Revenue (Worldwide): $25.96 million
2005 Total Firm Net Income (Worldwide): $7.67 billion
No. of Employees (Private Wealth): 8,000
No. of Employees (Firmwide): 52,000
No. of Office Locations (Worldwide): 2,388

Hiring Process

Recruiting

Wells Fargo recruits at numerous campuses throughout the U.S.

Hiring

Please describe the hiring process at your firm.

The interview process varies according to division and position. Candidates might go through telephone, group and/or individual interviews.

Does your firm offer summer internships?

Yes, and also during the academic year. See the firm's web site for details on which divisions offer them.

Visit Vault at **www.vault.com** for insider company profiles, expert advice,
career message boards, expert resume reviews, the Vault Job Board and more.

VAULT CAREER LIBRARY **221**

Inside the Firm: Culture and Training

Please describe the corporate culture at your firm.

Wells Fargo's slogan is "Mind share plus heart share equals market share." The firm relies on its employees to be its "competitive advantage" in its "journey" towards being one of the U.S.A.'s "great companies."

Please describe any mentoring programs at your firm.

The firm offers a private client services mentoring program.

Please describe any ongoing or other training programs for employees:

Goal-setting and performance education, online career development resources, tuition reimbursement for career-related courses.

Compensation

Please describe compensation and other monetary benefits at your firm.

Paid time off, matched 401(k) plan, team member financial package, stock purchase plan and spending accounts, among other offerings.

Please describe other perks.

Wellness benefits, commuter benefits, tuition reimbursement, adoption reimbursement, scholarships for dependent children, team member discount center, employee assistance consulting, long-term care, LifeCare resources and Weight Watchers reimbursement program, among others.

Diversity

Please describe any diversity hiring efforts in regards to minorities.

Wells Fargo cooperates with the Asian Pacific Island American Scholarship Fund, National Black MB Association, Hispanic Scholarship Fund, National Hispana Leadership Institute, National Hispanic Business Association and National Society of Hispanic MBAs.

William Blair Wealth Management

<table>
<tr><td>

222 West Adams Street
Chicago, IL 60606
Phone: (312) 236-1600
www.wmblair.com

**EMPLOYMENT
CONTACT**

E-mail: info@williamblair.com

See "careers" section of
www.williamblair.com

</td><td>

Chairman: Edgar D. Jannotta
CEO: John R. Ettelson
Firm Type: Private Company
**No. of Employees (Private
Brokerage):** 73
No. of Employees (Firmwide):
900
**No. of Office Locations
(Worldwide):** 8

</td></tr>
</table>

Hiring Process

Recruiting

The career page of the firm's web site lists job opportunities searchable by job category and location. Interested candidates are invited to submit a resume and application online.

Hiring

What are some of the requirements for jobs?

In the private investor department, bright people thrive. Individual ideas are recognized and autonomy is encouraged. But you won't be alone. Our resources are extensive, and with all of our investment professionals located in Chicago, you'll have access to them every day. All of our professionals also benefit from frequent industry best practices sessions.

Inside the Firm: Culture and Training

Please describe the corporate culture at your firm.

William Blair & Company believes in independence. We are one of the last independent, employee-owned investment firms. Our culture is entrepreneurial. We look for people who can take responsibility and put our clients' needs first—true professionals with integrity. Our philosophy has created a stable, collegial environment that the world's top professionals are drawn to and thrive in.

In the communities that William Blair & Company serves, you'll find our people helping out. Some of the organizations we are involved with are Christmas in April, Take your Daughters and Sons to Work Day, the American Heart Association, the Chase Corporate Challenge and the United Way.

Compensation

Please describe compensation and other monetary benefits at your firm.

William Blair's profit sharing includes a 401(k) plan in which you may defer at most 25 percent of your salary (up to $10,500). However, employees eligible for contributions from the firm may elect to defer salary up to only 21.5 percent of earnings in excess of $25,000. In addition, each plan year the firm generally will make contributions based out of its net profit.

Please describe other perks.

The firm offers 75 percent discounted commissions on trades. Various other discounts are available at restaurants, museums, parks and retailers. Employees are also eligible for tax-free spending accounts for health and commuter expenses.

Additional Information

Wealth management professionals at William Blair are dedicated to serving high-net-worth clients and endowments by providing independent, comprehensive and objective financial planning and consulting. We develop trusted, long-term relationships with clients, whereby we operate with a thorough understanding of goals, preferences and unique circumstances. As such, our advisory services are highly customized for every individual's needs.

Proprietary money management is the firm's core competency. For our high-net-worth investing clients, we make use of our global institutional platform of investment products, with the integration of key groups of experts—including financial planning, corporate and executive services, mutual funds and private capital—in addition to the network of outside money managers in a flexible architecture format.

The flexibility we offer allows us to tailor financial solutions to the specific needs of our clients. Decisions are driven by our clients' objectives and William Blair's unwavering dedication to helping our clients succeed. Our commitment to performance and superior service is the hallmark of our relationship with private clients.

The service lines within the wealth management group are financial planning, private brokerage, executive services, mutual funds and private capital. The financial planning division serves clients through estate and income tax planning, retirement planning, education funding, investment asset allocation, consolidated financial statements, insurance and risk management, employee stock option analysis and equity risk management strategies.

Visit the Vault Finance Career Channel at **www.vault.com/finance** — with
insider firm profiles, message boards, the Vault Finance Job Board and more.

V/\ULT CAREER LIBRARY   **225**

Appendix

Private Wealth Management Resources

Job Boards

Your best bet for job openings is to look directly at the postings on a given company's web site. However, there are a few others you may wish to consider:

www.jobsinthemoney.com

This job board's search engine has a field devoted to private banking, and the results are targeted and impressive in scope, from entry-level to managing director positions.

jobs.efinancialcareers.com/Private_Banking_%7C_Wealth_Management.htm

Part of the eFinancialCareers.com site, you'll see a wide variety of private wealth management or global private client job offerings from both large and small firms. These tend to be more senior positions, and they're often mixed in with asset management and other jobs.

www.vault.com/jobs/jobboard/searchform.jsp

We may have a particular bias for the Vault.com job boards, but you'll find a wide variety of job postings on the Vault Finance Job Board, including wealth management jobs. A search for "private banking" or "wealth management" on our boards will give you the latest openings.

Company Sites

To save time, use the link below for a list of private wealth management firms that are members of the Institute for Private Investors. The list offers links to individual firms' web sites: www.memberlink.net/memberlinkpublic /advmem/FR-advme.html

Visit the Vault Finance Career Channel at **www.vault.com/finance** – with
insider firm profiles, message boards, the Vault Finance Job Board and more.

VAULT CAREER LIBRARY   227

Industry Sites

www.memberlink.net/memberlinkpublic

Run by the Institute for Private Investors, this site is primarily a resource for high-net-worth individuals dealing with the interaction between themselves and investment advisors. However, it is generally insightful about trends in the industry, and dozens of private wealth management firms are members of the Institute.

www.thewealthnet.com/page_magazine.php

A British site, but with interesting insights into the growing industry, along with articles about upcoming trends and business developments.

www.pwmnet.com

The online adjunct to *Professional Wealth Management* magazine, another European product, this site features a strong focus on different types of investments and portfolio strategies, rather than about the business of private banking. However, there are some articles about careers in professional wealth management that are often eye-opening.

Regulatory Sites

www.nasd.com

Like anyone else involved in investing, private bankers and their activities come under the regulatory aegis of the National Association of Securities Dealers (NASD) and are generally considered broker-dealers, much like your average broker, and while there may be a handful of esoteric regulations that deal with private wealth management, most experts say private banks and wealth management firms are treated much the same as your local TD Ameritrade or Schwab branch.

About the Author

Mike Martinez is a 10-year veteran of business journalism whose coverage of Wall Street appears in newspapers around the globe. He is a former editor at *Kiplinger's Personal Finance* and author of *Practical Tech for Your Business*.

Visit the Vault Finance Career Channel at **www.vault.com/finance** – with
insider firm profiles, message boards, the Vault Finance Job Board and more.

VAULT CAREER LIBRARY   229

Decrease your T/NJ Ratio
(Time to New Job)

Use the Internet's most targeted job search tools for finance professionals.

Vault Finance Job Board

The most comprehensive and convenient job board for finance professionals. Target your search by area of finance, function, and experience level, and find the job openings that you want. No surfing required.

VaultMatch Resume Database

Vault takes match-making to the next level: post your resume and customize your search by area of finance, experience and more. We'll match job listings with your interests and criteria and e-mail them directly to your inbox.